EL PRESIDIO
de
San Diego

EL PRESIDIO *de* *San Diego*

Excavating Southern California's Lost City

Richard L. Carrico

THE History PRESS

Published by The History Press
An imprint of Arcadia Publishing
Charleston, SC
www.historypress.com

First published 2025

Manufactured in the United States

ISBN 9781467159616
Hardcover ISBN 9781540299888

Library of Congress Control Number: 2025941477

This book is dedicated to Paul H. Ezell and Greta Ezell. They strove for decades to bring the buried and largely forgotten Presidio de San Diego to life. Their efforts included archaeological excavation, archival research on primary Spanish documents, report preparation and the training of literally hundreds of students. Two sometimes disparate groups must also be part of any dedication: first, the Indigenous Kumeyaay and other tribal members who lived and worked at the presidio, and second, the Hispanic/ Californio settlers, soldiers and colonists who lived and in some cases died at the presidio. For both groups, the descendants of these people maintain a strong attachment to the ruins and the history of the presidio. While for most of us the ruins may well be California's Lost City, for these descendants, the presidio was never forgotten, never just a ruin, never lost.

CONTENTS

PREFACE

Growing up in San Diego, I experienced Presidio Hill at many levels, but none of them were academic or through a lens of historicity. As a preteen, my buddies and I would ride our tricked-out bicycles down to the park from East San Diego and use the grass-covered mounds as ramps to launch ourselves into the air. If you got enough speed, you might be able to jump over the next mound before taking to the air again.

In the winter—yes, San Diego experiences its own version of winter—and some mornings, the grassy lumps were covered in frost. Grabbing cardboard appliance boxes from a Mission Hills store, we would slice them into makeshift sleds and ride them from the top of the hill all the way to the bottom. Only much later did I learn that my frosty rides took me over the first Catholic church in Alta California and across the ultimate resting place of Spaniards, Native Americans and Americans.

Later, as a teenager with a '52 Ford, my visits to the park were always with a girl to watch what we called the "submarine races." There were no submarines, no races, only heavy petting in the backseat. We were told that the young lady had to keep her shoes on in case the cops came upon us. What? Well, apparently shoes on meant nothing too sexual was going on. Shoes off—well, who knows. Decades later, when I got married on the grass on top of the Spanish ruins, I thought back to those long-ago times. In the years between bicycle ramp jumps and making out in the parking lot above the ruins, I came to know the fascinating archaeology and history of Presidio Hill in ways that few others could.

Those of us who toiled away, excavating at the San Diego Presidio, grew accustomed to tourists and visitors lining the chain-link fence and asking questions. The people on the other side of the fence were from all over the world speaking a variety of languages. Some seemed enthralled to be witnessing archaeology in action. Visitors from Spain seemed fascinated to be on the site of one of their colonies.

Besides the usual "Did you find any gold yet?" was the more typical "What did you find?" question. The inquisitor did not want to know what an artifact weighed or at what depth an object was found. They wanted to know what the coolest thing was that we found. What was the oldest? Who was that skeleton? Who lived here, and was this really California's first mission?

This book can't answer every question, but it can give readers a better understanding of what archaeologists do and what we find. It can explain what artifacts tell us about the people who went before us. It can, we hope, make the ruins on Presidio Hill come alive, be more meaningful and anchor its place among Southern California's important landmarks. The challenge is to tell the story without getting too far into the weeds, without too many metrics or specific details that, frankly, may ruin the story for many readers.

Although based on over fifty years of research, this book is not footnoted or filled with quotations. For those who may want to pursue topics of interest further, the bibliography at the end of the book provides scores of academic sources for a wealth of details and analyses. A glossary of Spanish words and terms, some of which are arcane and not in current use, is provided at the rear of the book.

Artifacts, tile floors, animal bone and other detritus from the past have stories to tell, probably more stories than we will ever understand. But even in scratching the surface, we uncover lost worlds, persons long deceased and cultures often shrouded in mystery. Archaeology at historic sites sometimes uncovers unknown or unsaid truths. Archaeology can partially fill in the thoughts and actions left unwritten in official documents.

The story of the San Diego Presidio and its occupants is more than a tale about a single military fortification. It is a history of one of the western United States' first settlements in a region claimed by Spain. It is the story of Native resistance, feuds between the Franciscan missionaries and the Spanish military and a frontier outpost on the edge of the Pacific Ocean. It is in this context that we gain a better understanding of how the Native Kumeyaay people interacted with the Spaniards, how they adapted and how, despite drastic changes to the landscape and the scourge of introduced diseases, they persisted.

It is always at the forefront of the author's mind that archaeologists are foremost anthropologists. Or at least we should be. Too often researchers have dwelled on material objects, be they hat pins, bottle fragments or an entire adobe wall. While those things can often provide useful information about the past, they are rarely direct or accurate reflections of the people who used them or lost or discarded them. The goal of this book is to bring life to the men and women and, yes, children who inhabited the past at the San Diego Presidio. These people were, after all, alive, like you and me. They did far more than discard artifacts and food scraps for us to ponder. They left us chapters of their life stories and of early California history.

A note on the usage of ethnic, tribal and "racial" terms. In general, but not universally, the Native people within the United States have rejected the term "Indian" as an ethnic or racial term to describe them. Given the hundreds of tribes in the United States, there is no consensus of term or designation that should be used. At the tribal level, most would prefer the traditional name of their tribe, i.e., Kumeyaay, Lakota or Ojibway. When speaking of larger groups of tribes, or if a specific tribe cannot be determined, many linguists and scholars might use First People or Indigenous people. The term "Native American," which rose to some prominence after the 1970s, is viewed less favorably than in past decades.

For the Spanish Europeans who colonized and settled the San Diego region, what they should be called is sometimes even more vexing. Few of the settlers were actually from Spain, and many were generations removed and genetically distant from their Iberian Spanish roots. However, the people were indeed living in Nueva España (New Spain), swore at least some allegiance to a Spanish king, spoke the Spanish language (although that language was rapidly becoming New World Spanish) and practiced what might be called a Hispanic culture. They categorized themselves as *gente de razon*, people of reason. Within that larger group of Spaniards or Hispanics, a large percentage of them fell into ethnic (often mistakenly called racial) categories. These *castas*, such as mestizo, or color quebrado or coyote, reflect real or fictive blood lines traced to Black or Indigenous ancestors. What one called themselves might shift over time, with some individuals increasingly losing their "non-Hispanic" bloodlines and becoming less Black or less Indigenous.

Like the English American colonists on the East Coast, the Spanish colonists in Alta (Upper) California were moving away from their mother language, mainland Mexico cuisine and lifeways. The Catholic Church still formed a touchstone for the settlers, but even that venerable institution was transforming in the 1700s. So, in this book, mostly, the settlers and colonists at the presidio will be called Spaniards or Hispanics in contrast to the Native people and, later in time, the Americans. The term *Californios* will be used for most of San Diego's non-Indigenous population after the Mexican Revolution of 1821. Throwing off the shackles of Spain and Mexico, the Californias became something different than Nueva España. Its people living in what is now California increasingly saw themselves as independent, unique and Californian, i.e., they proudly became Californios.

ACKNOWLEDGEMENTS

As always, the first acknowledgement for my work on early San Diego history must go to Paul and Greta Ezell. They inspired me, criticized me and, as they did with so many of their students, made me a better person and scholar. The extraordinary research conducted on ceramics from the presidio by Stephen Van Wormer, Susan Walter and Sue Wade contributed to the backbone of all discussions of ceramics in this book. They brought clarity on the topic of ceramics and trade. Two of the hand-drawn illustrations are the wonderful work of my colleague Harry Price.

Jaime Lennox, director of collections at San Diego State University, where the thousands of artifacts from the university's presidio excavations are curated, greatly assisted with allowing access to the thousands of pages of logbook entries and the artifacts themselves. Steven Freers greatly assisted me in ensuring that many of the graphic illustrations in the book are of publishable quality. Samantha Ely, archivist at the San Diego city clerk's office, assisted with access to data from previous excavations.

Several people and institutions shared their photographs and images, including Josh McNair of See California Through My Lens, the San Diego Maritime Museum, the Amon Carter Museum of American Art, the Bancroft Library at Berkeley, the San Diego History Center, the Ramona Pioneer Historical Society and the National Archives.

Stan Berryman and Ronald V. May, past project directors at the presidio, provided photographs and insights into their work there. The previous excavations by Paul Ezell, Diane Barbolla, Jack Williams and Brad Bartel all contributed to the immense collection of artifacts and faunal remains from the settlement. The late Jack Williams deserves special attention for all his research on primary documents, his dedication to archaeology and his willingness to share his research.

Past and present staff at the San Diego History Center include the late Colonel John Ellis, who served as a site steward for several years and allowed access to many previously unpublished photographs. Robert Jackson of Mexico City and a preeminent scholar of Spanish borderlands and mission history offered insights to terms and objects, shared photographs and brought forth myriad other aspects of early Spanish colonial culture. Lee Panich of Santa Clara University has always been an excellent source for all things mission related. I gratefully acknowledge Jesse Pinto, Jamul Tribal chairwoman Erica Pinto and other members of the Kumeyaay community for their ceaseless efforts to track down the story of their people at the presidio and, in some cases, the final resting places of their ancestors.

Chapter 1

FIRST PEOPLE

Thousands of years before Spanish colonists settled in what is now San Diego, the region was occupied by Native groups. The earliest accepted archaeological manifestation of Native Americans in the San Diego area has been called the San Dieguito complex, dating to approximately twelve thousand years ago. This does not mean that Indigenous people have been in the region only back to that date. It simply reflects the earliest verifiable date for human occupation—older sites will certainly be discovered.

Dates for human occupation of the Americas and Southern California in particular are continually being pushed further and further back in time. Given advancing sea levels over the past twelve thousand years, the oldest archaeological sites may be beyond our immediate reach—under the Pacific Ocean. The people of this period (twelve thousand to nine thousand years ago) were largely nomadic, meaning they apparently did not establish permanent settlements, although they may have returned to favored sites on occasion. The burial patterns, language and other important cultural traits are uncertain for the people of this period.

The material culture of the San Dieguito complex, or First People, consists primarily of scrapers, scraper planes, choppers, large blades and large projectile points. Finely crafted crescentic stones used for uncertain purposes may also be characteristic of the San Dieguito complex. Tools and debitage (debris from making or maintaining stone tools) made of fine-grained green metavolcanic material, locally known as felsite or metavolcanic, were found at many sites that are identified as San Dieguito. Both the finished artifacts

Precontact San Dieguito complex stone knife blades from the C.W. Harris site, circa 9500 BCE. *Author's collection.*

and the debitage offer important clues as to manufacturing techniques, tool function and even cultural preference for one type of stone over another.

Often these artifacts are heavily patinated, meaning they have an outer rind or cortex reflecting thousands of years of weathering and mineral buildup. Metavolcanic tools, especially patinated felsite, came to be seen as an indicator of the San Dieguito complex. This assumption is no longer accepted at face value. Researchers now realize that several factors can affect the degree of patination, not just time.

The types of artifacts (knife blades, spear points and large scrapers) associated with the San Dieguito are consistent with a people who hunted and processed large to medium game. This may have included ground sloths, antelope and mammoths. Until relatively recently, many archaeologists believed that the San Dieguito culture lacked milling technology for the processing of seeds and grains. They saw this as an important difference between the San Dieguito and later complexes. It is now more accepted that in the later stages of the San Diego complex, some level of milling occurred.

Sleeping circles, trail shrines and rock alignments in the eastern deserts have also been associated with early San Dieguito sites. At one time, a

Colorado River with the Quechan. While there is no general agreement on the meaning of the word *Kumeyaay*, it most likely means "people of the coast" or "people of the coastal cliffs." Agua Hedionda Lagoon, thirty miles north of the presidio, near Carlsbad, California, is often described as the division between the Kumeyaay and tribes to the north to include the Luiseño.

In the immediate area of what would become the San Diego Presidio and Mission Valley, the Kumeyaay lived in large settlements containing populations that varied from fifty to two hundred individuals. These villages were autonomous, each having their own set of military, religious and political leaders. The overall population of the Kumeyaay at the time of Spanish intrusion has been estimated at between fifteen thousand and twenty thousand. From these villages, the people accessed the nearby coast and, to the east, the more distant mountains and out to the deserts.

Not just simple hunter-gatherers, the Kumeyaay practiced an elaborate system of land management and food procurement. Major food sources were acorns, buckwheat, chia, deer, rabbits, shellfish and ocean fish. The Kumeyaay did not domestic plants but did practice proto agriculture,

Kumeyaay woman at Kwellemak (Capitan Grande) winnowing acorns. Note the various basket types used in the process. *Ramona Pioneer Historical Society.*

which refers to transplanting useful plants for food or medicine, often in environments where such plants would not have been endemic. Examples would include certain varieties of cactus and elderberry for teas. They fished in the bays and offshore in tule boats made of reeds and occasionally from dugout canoes. The islands to the north and Los Coronados to the south were frequently visited in search of abalone and shallow-water fish.

The Kumeyaay had a well-developed sense of the cosmos around them, including astronomical objects such as the planets and major stars. They marked the changing seasons from a series of solstice and equinox observatories on one of four or five major peaks, including Kuuchamaa on what is now the Mexican border and Viejas Peak in eastern San Diego County. Expert astronomers, the Kumeyaay strategically painted images on prominent boulders to delineate the passage of the sun, moon and Venus in the sky. Sky phenomena meant more than just objects in the skies. Some Kumeyaay groups believe that the sparks and ashes from human cremations rise into the skies to join their ancestors in the Milky Way.

On the land, the Kumeyaay practiced fire science, using controlled burns to reduce the danger of fire and renew and replenish native plant communities. Periodical burns would destroy parasites, reduce fuel loads and ensure bountiful crops of pine nuts, which require fire to explode their cones. As recorded by early Spanish explorers, such burns were also used as a hunting method to drive rabbits and deer toward hunters and hunting blinds.

In Kumeyaay oral tradition, *Sinyohauch*, the First Mother, told one of her sons that one way to hunt deer was to set fire to mountain grasses where the deer live, and he will run down to you. Kumeyaay women manufactured a variety of free-form paddle and anvil pottery forms known as Tizon Brown Ware. Examples of this ware were abundant in the archaeological discoveries at the presidio. The women also wove tightly constructed baskets from juncus and sumac fibers, sometimes weaving designs into the fiber.

Singing and dancing were, and still are, important elements of Kumeyaay spiritual and social life. Several of the traditional Kumeyaay songs, which are still sung today, tell of the creation of the land and the people. Others are travelogues describing Kumeyaay lands far and near. An extensive set of trails linked the coastal Kumeyaay with their cousins on the Colorado River and far south into Baja California. Several of these trails became major travel corridors for Spanish explorers and colonists. In many places, El Camino Real (the Royal or King's Highway) followed ancient Native trails.

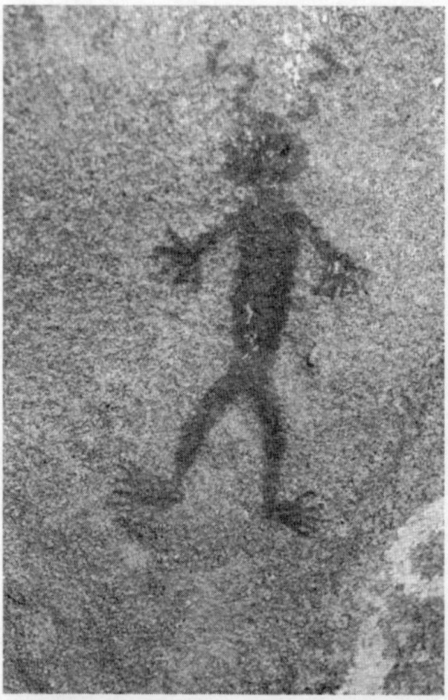

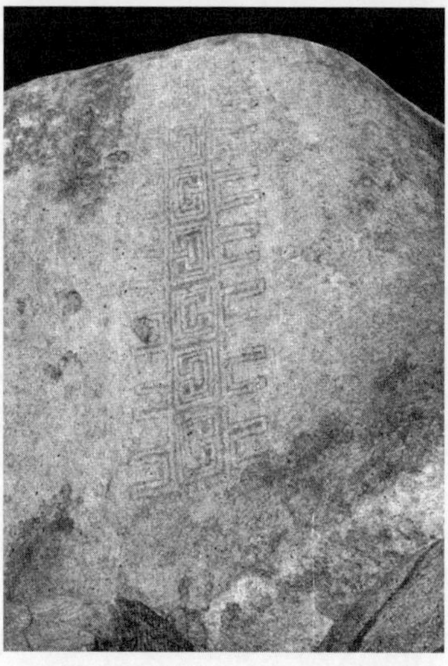

Above, left: Sunwatcher winter solstice marker at Vallecitos de La Rumorosa, Baja California. *Ken Hedges.*

Above, right: Finely woven sumac and juncus fiber basket woven by María Cuero. *Imperial Valley Desert Museum.*

Left: "Maze" design pictograph at Rancho Bernardo, California. Similar pictographs have been dated to 1200 BCE. *Ken Hedges.*

The Kumeyaay, like all the Indigenous people of North America, did not possess a written language until after Spanish contact. Instead, they conveyed thoughts, events and spiritual meanings by way of singing, rock paintings (pictographs) and carvings (petroglyphs). Although the meanings of some of the more abstract paintings and carvings may be inscrutable to non-Native viewers, they held great meaning to the creators and observers.

It was these Kumeyaay people for whom Mission San Diego de Alcalá was built in hopes of converting them to Catholicism and, in the process, making the San Diego region into a viable Spanish colony. It was also these people for whom the San Diego Presidio was built to protect the new colony and the expanding Spanish frontier from these Native people. Certainly, Russia's and England's territorial expansions concerned the governments in Spain and Mexico City. But the military focus was to protect the infant colony from the local, Indigenous people.

Chapter 2

SPAIN EXPANDS INTO ALTA CALIFORNIA

The economic and political forces that led to the Spanish settlement of San Diego were forged in faraway Spain and Mexico City. In the more than two hundred years since Spanish forces subdued the Aztec empire and colonized Mexico City, Nueva España, or New Spain, had spread far and wide. Large portions of what is now Mexico sprouted settlements and colonies. On the East Coast of America, Florida and the Caribbean Islands to the south became Spanish strongholds.

San Diego, known previously as San Miguel, was visited by Juan Rodríguez Cabrillo in 1542. It is unclear what effect his visit may have had on the local Native population. It is possible that some strains of European-based diseases may have been introduced to the Native population at this time. Cabrillo and others reported that the harbor, the natural resources and the climate made the area an excellent spot for a colony or settlement. In later decades, the harbor took the name San Diego in honor of Saint Didacus.

Following decades of settlement in mainland Mexico and Baja California, Catholic missionaries and military forces pushed northward into Alta (Upper) California. Close on the heels of the expulsion of Jesuit adherents from Mexico in 1769, Franciscan missionaries led by Father Junípero Serra accompanied by naval and army forces began their movement into Alta California. This initial thrust into the uncharted lands was accomplished by both land forces moving up the Baja California peninsula and naval

Replica of Juan Cabrillo's sailing ship the *San Salvador*. *San Diego Maritime Museum/Bobby Grieser.*

forces sailing up the Pacific side. There were supposed to be three heavily laden ships to supply the new colony, but only two made it to San Diego harbor. This failure to adequately supply the new settlement would be repeated for decades.

Arrival in 1769 of Spanish colonists composed of Franciscan missionaries, soldiers, sailors, muleteers and craftsmen marked a significant and seminal event in the long history of Alta California. Ultimately, four presidios, or forts, would be established in Alta California: one each at San Diego, Monterey, San Francisco and Santa Barbara. These four military installations became Spanish settlements apart from the twenty-one missions. They served as the administrative centers, often housed territorial governors and included prisons for both Spaniards and Native people.

From a small camp along the bay, Father Serra and army officers Gaspar de Portolá and Fernando Rivera y Moncada moved to higher ground on what became known as Presidio Hill. Father Serra was left with a small band of soldiers as Portolá and Rivera trekked on to explore the northern regions. They specifically were looking for Monterey Bay, the proposed site for a large mission and presidio. In the absence of senior military leaders,

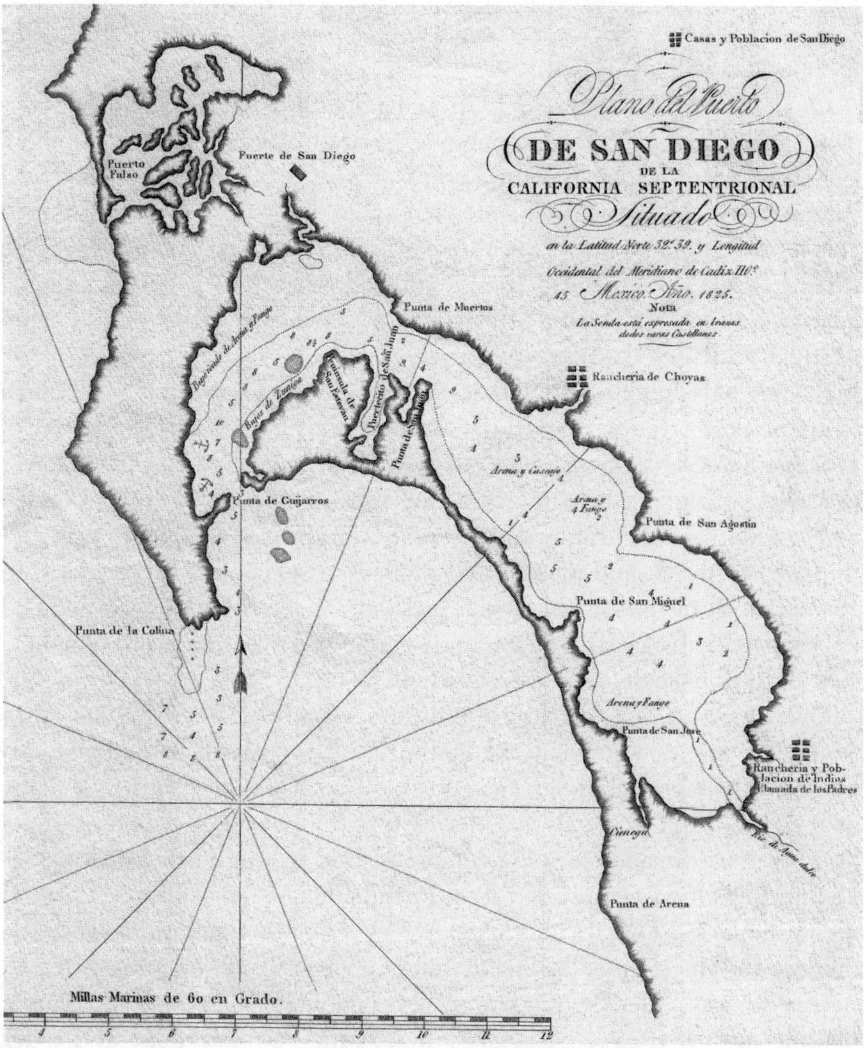

Pantoja's 1782 map of San Diego Bay and the region. Note the presidio is shown north of San Diego Bay. *Bancroft Library, Berkeley, California.*

on July 16, 1769, Father Serra raised a crudely hewn wooden cross on the nearly barren hill, thus founding Mission San Diego de Alcalá. From this inauspicious beginning, the San Diego Presidio and mission began.

Within three months of their arrival, the small contingent of Spaniards were besieged by discontented Kumeyaay warriors. It had become obvious to the villagers at Kosaii at the foot of Presidio Hill that the newcomers intended to stay. Additionally, the Spaniards had little to offer the Kumeyaay.

In Kumeyaay culture, visitors to their territory were expected to bring gifts to show goodwill and reciprocity.

One of the major items sought from the Spaniards by the Kumeyaay was cloth. When Serra and his companions told the village leaders that no more cloth would be provided to them, a group of Kumeyaay sailors launched reed canoes and attacked the *San Carlos* anchored in the harbor. The disgruntled Native men attempted to slash the canvas sails and take them as overdue tribute. They were repelled by on-board guards. In response, additional guards were sent to the ship for protection, leaving the little Spanish camp nearly defenseless.

In August 1769, realizing that most of the soldiers had gone north with Portolá or were on board the *San Carlos*, insurgents led by a powerful *kwaapaay* named Naguasajo attacked Serra's little encampment. In what was described as a pitched battle, several persons on both sides were wounded and one young Spanish boy, a valet or servant, from Guadalajara was shot through the throat and killed. Ironically, seven years later, Serra met with Naguasajo in his prison cell at the presidio. Naguasajo had been arrested for his part in the sacking of the mission in November 1775. He remained steadfastly anti-Spaniard and recalcitrant.

Over the next several months and then years, expeditions to the north continued, and new missions were established at Carmel, Padua and San Gabriel. Short on supplies, threatened by local Kumeyaay and with many of the sailors and soldiers still suffering from scurvy, the new outpost hung by a tenuous thread. From his command post to the north in Monterey, Lieutenant Pedro Fages bristled at the thought that he was expected to protect the missionaries. This set the stage for decades of competition between the military and the church, leading at times to outright animosity.

For five years, the new settlers toiled on the hill to build a small church, housing for the troops, bastions to mount their two cannons and other elements of the fort. The term presidio, derived from *presidium*, meaning "to preside," was applied to the settlement although it was not officially recognized as a royal presidio for several more years. Under Spanish law, the presidio and especially the mission were expected to fend for themselves, with only limited support from the Spanish government in Mexico City more than eighteen hundred miles to the south and San Blas thirteen hundred miles distant. The priests and colonists were instructed to grow their own crops; raise successful herds of cattle, pigs and horses; and defend the little hillside settlement from Native and foreign forces. For the first year, the military element consisted of fewer than ten ill-equipped men.

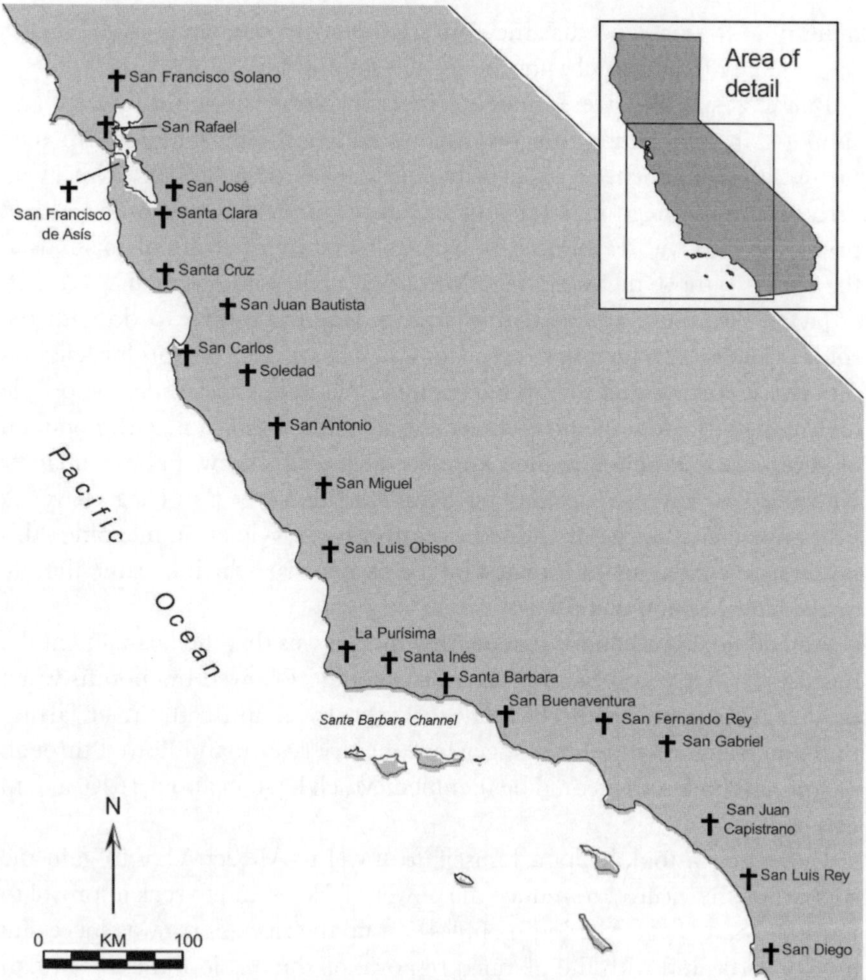

The twenty-one Franciscan missions of Alta California. *Lee Panich, Santa Clara University.*

The fort and mission within it expanded sporadically and slowly. The soldiers did not believe it was their role to serve as laborers and certainly not as unpaid workers for the church. They did, however, work as wage earners as tailors, teachers, blacksmiths, laborers and tile fabricators. Local Kumeyaay workers and Native people brought up from Baja California refused to work without being paid and fed. After the mission relocated farther east in 1774, the mission priest, Luis Jayme, believed that able-bodied Native men should devote their efforts to building that mission. Further, the priests told the military at the presidio that the converted Natives (neophytes) were under the domain of the church, not the secular authorities.

Building supplies were scarce, especially large trees for beams and supports, thus impeding the construction. Yet by the third and fourth year, the presidio settlement was taking shape. As it was forming, Luis Jayme, who arrived in San Diego in 1771 and served as the newly appointed resident priest, pleaded with Father Serra, who was founding a string of missions to the north, to move the San Diego Mission away from the presidio.

Jayme's rationale was that the Natives wanted nothing to do with the soldiers and were reluctant to come into the palisades of the fort for religious services. Realizing that the Spaniards had little to offer or trade, the people of Kosaii, at the foot of the hill, were rapidly developing a negative opinion of these bearded men and their animals. Jayme also knew that much larger Native settlements were located farther inland along the San Diego River. A primary village that Jayme hoped to convert was Nyip'ewai, meaning "this house here" (Nipaguay as spelled by the Spaniards), which became the site of the later Mission San Diego.

An additional reason for moving the mission was that the farmland at the base of the hill was subject to seasonal flooding followed by months when there was no water in the San Diego River. By contrast, the river farther upstream retained moisture longer into the dry season and flowed through narrow landforms that could be dammed. Much later, in about 1815, a dam was built upriver.

Father Serra took it upon himself to travel to Mexico City to gain the support of the viceroy, to reduce the power of Fages and to seek approval to move the San Diego Mission six miles east up the river. Serra was successful in his efforts, and with the planned removal of the mission, the fort at San Diego was officially declared a royal presidio on January 1, 1774. In May of that year, the mission and its priests resettled on a gradual hill above a fertile floodplain. San Diego now consisted of a military installation at the presidio and a religious one at the mission. The pole and brush *pobre choza* (reed hut) church at the presidio gradually fell into ruin and ultimately burned. Among the troops and their officers, there was little effort given toward building a proper chapel. Despite the reluctance, short brown adobe walls soon replaced the religious hut and would later serve as the skeleton for the much larger church.

On November 4, 1775, eighteen months after establishment of the new mission, rebel warriors from about eighteen Tipai settlements south of the San Diego River attacked it. The Tipai burned the partially constructed adobe and brush church to the ground. The attack on the newly established mission was a startling setback for the Spanish colonists. Father Luis Jayme and two craftsmen were killed, religious icons were stolen and the mission was destroyed. Later, under severe interrogation, several of the rebel leaders said that their holy men feared the new religion. In his recently successful efforts at making converts, Father Jayme had been seen as a demon, a malignant spiritual force who must be killed. While the Tipai held the military at the presidio in disdain, their goal had not been to destroy them. It was the demon and the sacrilegious temple that they were after. In that, they succeeded.

New forces were sent to San Diego, including twenty-five Catalonian recruits who came from mainland San Blas by way of ship. The palisades at the presidio were reinforced, and the settlement at San Diego seemed on the brink of failure. The presidio, which seemed always short on supplies, now had an influx of soldiers swelling its garrison to over one hundred. The intrepid Father Serra refused to abandon San Diego, as suggested by military authorities, and within a year personally took on the task of rebuilding the mission.

While a new second mission was under construction upriver with a labor force composed partially of sailors from the sailing ship *Principle*, improvements within the presidio continued. The presidio construction included living quarters for the priests and apparently raising wooden facades above the adobe walls on the dilapidated church. Whether or not this structure constituted a formal church later became a hotly contested issue. A cobblestone-floored prison with thick adobe walls was hastily built.

Following the destruction of the mission, Kumeyaay men and women were brought to the presidio, interrogated and imprisoned. At one point, there were more than twenty Native prisoners held in shackles in the prison. The interrogations were overseen by Captain Fernando Rivera y Moncada, who advocated ample application of whips.

Rivera strongly advocated exile of the prisoners to San Blas, where they would be assigned to hard labor. Serra, on the other hand, pleaded for Christian mercy, believing it would lead to peace among the Kumeyaay. Both men knew that Spanish forces were greatly outnumbered by the Kumeyaay. Ultimately, most of the prisoners were released back to their Native villages but warned that if there were any further violence toward the Spaniards, there would be swift reprisals.

One of the Christian rebel leaders, Carlos, came to the presidio and sought sanctuary in the church. He sought to have Father Vicente Fuster intervene on his behalf. Captain Rivera denied the plea for sanctuary and had Carlos forcibly removed from the building. Enraged, Father Fuster claimed that Rivera had broken church law and that the rebels deserved the grace of God. Rivera rejected the priest's pleas and threw Carlos in the dark and dank prison. In response, Father Fuster excommunicated the irate military leader, although Rivera was later reinstated.

This was once again an example of the tug-of-war going on between the church and crown. Ultimately, Carlos was released and told to remain peaceful or else he and his people would feel the wrath of Captain Moncada. Four years later, while leading a caravan of settlers and military personnel across the desert, Captain Rivera and most of his group, including two sergeants from the presidio garrison, were killed or taken hostage by Quechan (Yuma) Indians along the banks of the Colorado River near Yuma, Arizona.

In 1781, a twenty-year-old *soldado distinguido* (essentially a nobleman) and experienced frontier military commander, Lieutenant José de Zúñiga, took charge of the presidio. Zúñiga began an expansive building period. Using an approximately eighty-three-foot-by-twenty-foot rectangle of foundation stones and adobe blocks that had been started several years before, Zúñiga toiled to complete a more formal church. By 1783, Zúñiga had built a defensive adobe wall around the presidio, installed two bastions in the northwest and southeast corners of the fort, improved the soldiers' quarters and finished the first fully adobe church on the hill. Reportedly, he worked on the chapel as a painter, mason and carpenter.

This effort—which included digging hundreds of yards of foundation trenches, hauling large foundation stones up from the river, manufacturing unfired adobe bricks from adobe clay soils and making kiln-fired clay floor tiles—was performed largely by Native workers. Prisoners—both Spanish convicts and Indigenous inmates from the presidio prison—also provided manual labor. Known as *presidiarios* (convict laborers), convicted Californios from Baja California were sent to San Diego to serve their time.

Additionally, as commandant, Zúñiga could have enlisted the labor of some of his loyal soldiers as well as the resident blacksmith and carpenter. Most likely, the blacksmith and carpenter may have had Native apprentices and aides. Lacking an architect, Zúñiga no doubt relied on his knowledge of churches in his previous posts. He had served at several outposts in the Texas territory. Zúñiga perhaps also consulted the well-known book of architecture written by the Roman architect and engineer Vitruvius. Mission records indicate that the priests supplied Zúñiga with religious materials for the new church. Unlike his predecessors, the young officer gained the trust and friendship of the robed friars. Zúñiga served at the San Diego Presidio for eleven years until 1792.

Large timbered wood for the upright beams and major cross rafters were probably shipped down on supply ships from Monterey, where majestic forests were common. Smaller beams of oak, willow and pine were harvested in the mountains of eastern San Diego for construction at both the presidio and the mission. Local Kumeyaay oral tradition tells of Native laborers dragging the lumber down with the aid of oxen.

For most years, there was at least one carpenter on site for both large-scale woodworking and smaller projects. Inventories show that he and other artisans were supplied with saws, hammers, chisels and wood planes. For at least twenty-five years, master blacksmith Felipe Romero manufactured and repaired metal objects at the presidio. His tenure at the presidio was probably the longest of any of its occupants. During his time there, he buried his mother and at least two children.

When a census was made of the San Diego Presidio in 1790, the installation had swelled to 190 persons, including many married women and children. Zúñiga had ensured that better housing was provided for the soldiers, especially the married men. There were at least thirty-four families living in the small casitas built for men with wives and children. Only fourteen of the male occupants were single; one was a widower. The quarters must have been cramped; families with at least five children were not uncommon.

Gone were the simple brush and reed roofs, replaced with at least wattle and daub and in some cases adobe tiles. The adobe wall enclosing the approximately six-acre presidio had been reinforced, and most of the buildings were freshly whitewashed. Within the niches at the east end of the sanctuary above the altar, statues of Catholic saints adorned the walls. In many ways, the period from 1790 to 1810 marks the zenith of the San Diego Presidio. Turmoil and political upheaval in mainland Mexico would soon lead to the decay and ultimate abandonment of Alta California's first European settlement.

Chapter 3

MEXICAN INDEPENDENCE, ABANDONMENT AND DECAY

In the run-up to Mexican independence in 1821, small numbers of presidial soldiers retired from the military and planted the roots for what became the Pueblo de San Diego. After sometimes decades of poor pay and hard living conditions, these men and their families were ready for civilian life. Small plots of land at the base of the hill were available to retired soldiers. In later years, large land grants were given to officers and supporters of a governor. Those grants became the sprawling ranches and haciendas associated with what some writers call the "Zorro Period."

One of the first settlers to leave the presidio was Francisco María Ruiz, a past commandant of the presidio from 1809 to 1827. In about 1817, or perhaps earlier, he built a small adobe below the presidio. There, slightly above the floodplain, although it shifted occasionally, he planted a fruit orchard, including pears. Like many of the first settlers in the nascent pueblo, Ruiz and others who followed him planted and maintained small gardens to provide fresh fruits and vegetables for their families.

Ruiz gave the small adobe to a relative, Joaquin Carrillo, the father of Josefa Carrillo, who was later to be the wife of Henry Delano Fitch. This building still stands today, serving as a pro shop for a small golf course within the nine-hole Presidio Hills Golf Course. Appropriately, the golf course is not only the site of one of the oldest still-standing buildings in San Diego, but it was also founded by George Marston, the patron saint of presidio preservation.

With Mexican independence from Spain in 1821, the presidios of California lost much of their funding and support. The new Mexican government could not, or would not, provide supplies and economic support to the far-flung presidios in Alta California. While there were still the occasional Native uprisings, the presidios were not effective at ensuring peace. The pueblo of San Diego grew sporadically and slowly. The settlement had not gained the population or agricultural footing that other settlements such as San Gabriel, Santa Barbara and Sonoma had.

Troops were withdrawn, and the equipment was not replenished. Those soldiers who remained in San Diego moved out of the presidio and on to the broad plain at the foot of the hill. These men and their families founded what became the city of San Diego. One important leader who served at the presidio was José María Estudillo, who served twice as a commandant of the presidio. His large family adobe, built in 1827, is part of Old Town San Diego State Historic Park. For years, the venerable building was erroneously known as Ramona's Marriage Place to cash in on the popularity of Helen Hunt Jackson's epic tale of Ramona. Sugar magnate and operator of the streetcar system John D. Spreckels encouraged riders to visit the fictive marriage place. No matter that the fictional Ramona in the book and the real Ramona had never stepped a sandaled foot in San Diego. Today, after careful restoration, the Estudillo House annually receives thousands of visitors.

Junípero Serra Museum on Presidio Hill, San Diego. *Josh McNair/CaliforniaThroughMyLens.*

Within a decade of Mexican independence, the twenty-one California missions were ordered to be secularized and converted to chapels and dioceses serving the frontier Mexican pueblos and communities. Secularization ended California's so-called Mission Period. By 1835, all the Franciscan missionaries had been shipped out of Alta California. Within the San Diego Presidio, only a small squad of soldiers remained.

In 1835, and without a documented ceremony, the presidio was abandoned by troops who left for another assignment to the north. The last remnant of the presidial garrison marched north to San Gabriel near Los Angeles in 1835 and never returned. The final burial at the presidio in this period was José de la Luz Carrillo in November 1827. In 1848, José Francisco Snook and then Henry Delano Fitch (Enrique Domingo Fitch) in 1849 were buried at the presidio. They are the only two known Americans, later Mexican citizens, who are buried in consecrated ground at the presidio. Over the next few years, a few soldiers and officers who ventured down to San Diego occasionally stayed in the adjacent pueblo.

Yet for reasons not clear, on December 18, 1841, Bishop Francisco García Diego y Moreno offered the Sacrament of Confirmation to 125 persons at what must have been a forlornly desolate chapel. Perhaps his rationale for that location was that the mission was too remote from the pueblo. Assumedly, after roughly this date, burials of Mexican community members would have been at Mission San Diego or later, after 1849, at the Catholic campo santo in what became the Pueblo de San Diego.

Cessation of fighting in the Mexican War and the signing of the Treaty of Guadalupe Hidalgo in February 1848 heralded the start of American control of upper California. In the 1850s, the United States Army established a small garrison at Mission San Diego. The army apparently saw no use for the rapidly collapsing presidio. The old chapel was used to stable horses, and when they died, American soldiers joined the Natives, Spanish and Mexicans in the mission cemetery.

By the mid- to late 1840s, settlers in the pueblo at the bottom of the hill (now Old Town) had essentially looted the abandoned presidio in search of timber, fired clay tiles and anything useful. The two best sources for building material were probably the old commandant's house and the chapel, both of which had been better maintained than the other, smaller structures. After the American takeover of Alta California in 1848, the Pueblo de San Diego gradually became the village or town of San Diego.

The Californio or Mexican population played an important role in early San Diego. Some, however, had moved to more distant ranch lands, including some migration to Baja California. Today, several descendants of presidio soldiers live in northern Baja California. After Henry Fitch's passing, the remaining Fitch family moved to Healdsburg in Northern California. Henry Fitch had established a large rancho (Rancho Sotoyome) in what is now Sonoma County before his death.

San Diego became a pueblo populated by retired Mexican soldiers, Californios, Hispanic people from other regions, Native people and Anglo-Americans. Some of these citizens maintained Native American servants, including Juan Bandini, an immigrant from Peru who kept a large staff. An ill-fated Kumeyaay revolt in 1835 coincided with violence on the interior ranchos. In the backcountry, ranchos were sacked, hostages were taken and once again the Kumeyaay showed their persistence.

In the San Diego pueblo, the insurrection was quickly quelled by armed militia, resulting in the execution of several Native Americans on the southern edge of what became Old Town. Yet afterward, several Native men, perhaps Kumeyaay, were listed in the 1838 census as *pescadores* (fishermen). Some Native men also served as well-respected trackers and hunting guides. Native women, perhaps some from the presidio, worked as cooks, laundry women and nannies within the adobe homes.

With the establishment of a cemetery and Catholic church within the pueblo itself, there was little to draw San Diego's citizens up the hill to the largely forgotten and forlorn presidio. There were a few exceptions. In the 1870s, an unknown number of Native American men and women were buried in, or near, the abandoned cemetery next to the presidio chapel. The reasons for Native burial up on the hill are uncertain. Racism that excluded them from the pueblo's cemetery may have been a factor. Or it may have been that they had an emotional attachment to the presidio. Perhaps they had been married there, or bore a child there, or buried a child there.

Chapter 4

THE PAST BELONGS TO THE PEOPLE

After official abandonment in the late 1830s marked by occasional visits and burials in the 1840s and 1870s, including Henry Fitch and his daughter Natalia and the later unnamed Native people from Old Town, the presidio continued its steady slow slide into semi-oblivion. As part of an ill-fated effort to divert the San Diego River away from the town in 1853, George Derby got a contract to build a levee. He drafted a highly professional map of the San Diego River, the village of San Diego and the "Ruins of the Old Presidio." Often referred to as Derby's Dike, the construction depended on Native American laborers. Perhaps because of Kumeyaay reluctance to work on the project or the willingness of other tribes to do so, Kumeyaay may not have been involved.

Instead, Luiseño from North County, led by Manuel Cota, toiled as the primary labor force. Cota was a mixed-blood mestizo born to a Californio soldier and a Gabrieliño woman. Because Cota's men were from settlements fifty miles to the north, work sites were set up for them. The workers were housed in tents and rationed meals. To get solid fill dirt, Derby dynamited the most northerly portion of a cliff holding the already collapsing adobe barracks and family casitas.

A newspaper account of the demolition noted that human skulls and Spanish artifacts rained down on the riverbed and were quickly hauled off to form the dike. Whether the bones that fell from the old presidio were human (not likely, given its location away from the cemetery) or animal bones associated with the presidio residences is uncertain. One newspaper account noted that a large mill wheel fell from the bluffs. What is certain is that during the next rainy season, Derby's Dike broke open, and whatever Spanish treasures it contained washed around the foot of Presidio Hill and toward San Diego Bay.

By the 1920s, Presidio Hill and the rich history that it held were largely forgotten. The once thriving pueblo had been abandoned, and Alonzo Horton's "New Town" became central San Diego. The occasional picnickers might spend a leisurely Sunday afternoon up on the hill. Young couples occasionally snuck away from nearby homes for a few moments alone among the trees and brambles. Teenage boys from San Diego High School roamed the hills having pushing contests to see who could topple the tallest and largest adobe wall remnant. When their mischief was over, most walls were no taller than three feet.

The top of the hill set back from the old fort became expensive and sought-after property with names like Presidio Hills and Mission Hills. With expansive views of the bays and the ocean, the new Spanish-style homes became the residences of lawyers, bankers and other members of San Diego's elite. Most people believed it was only a matter of time before two-story mansions and elaborate formal gardens replaced the brown adobe lumps and coarse sands that cloaked the hill.

One of the prominent developers of parcels and residences above the old presidio was the local department store merchant George Marston. Beyond residential development, Marston had something in mind for the ruins themselves. As early as 1907, he and three of his equally or more wealthy cronies—John D. Spreckels the sugar mogul, A.G. Spaulding of sporting goods fame and E.W. Scripps, the publishing and media magnate—purchased almost fifty acres, including the presidio site, with plans to develop a public park with large custom homes on its outer edges.

Over the next two decades, Marston and a visionary planner, John Nolen, tried to convince the city to purchase the presidio site for public use and enjoyment. But then and now, city officials were reluctant to set aside parkland for fear of losing tax base and being stuck with maintenance costs. Interest in the old presidio site was also clouded by growing efforts to restore the still standing, although badly deteriorated mission structures at the San Diego Mission. Frustrated, Marston bought out his partners, giving them generous dividends on their initial investment.

By 1926, the San Diego common council and other officials had accepted the donation of almost fifty acres of prime land for use as a public park. To ensure that the history of the site would not be lost, Marston and others founded the San Diego Historical Society (now part of the San Diego History Center) and donated funds to build a museum above the old ruins. The stated intent was to further preserve the birthplace of European San Diego and, if possible, restore some of the old adobe buildings.

The museum, christened as the Junípero Serra Museum, would serve as the park's focal point from its prominent place on the hill's promontory. The museum was designed by noted Spanish Revival–style architect William Templeton Johnson. Locally, Johnson also designed the magnificent San Diego Natural History Museum in Balboa Park and the famed La Valencia Hotel in La Jolla, among other prominent buildings. Internationally, Johnson designed several buildings for the Ibero-American Exposition of 1929 in Seville, Spain.

During construction of the roads, irrigation and the museum itself, Percy Broell, a city gardener/landscaper, conducted semiprofessional archaeological excavations. His crew uncovered tile floors, remnants of the soldiers' barracks, and pulled Spanish and Mexican period artifacts from the ground. Broell accurately sketched the general construction techniques used in the late 1700s buildings. Some of the artifacts he recovered became the basis for the new museum's first artifact collections and displays. For some unknown reason, assumedly posterity, Broell constructed a wood frame or box encompassing one of the adobe bases that once supported a column in a doorway. Broell's maps and sketches would be used sixty years later to guide archaeologists in their searches. The History Center still

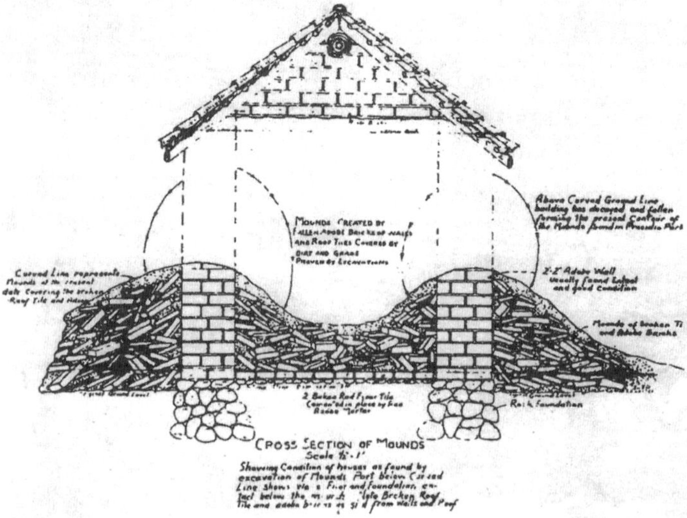

Percy Broell's sketch of presidio construction techniques. *San Diego History Center.*

Photo of Percy Broell's boxed pilaster base at baptistry entrance, circa 1928. *San Diego History Center.*

curates the Broell map and his notes as part of the extensive collection of presidio documents.

On July 16, 1929, the large, ornate wooden doors of the Spanish Revival–style Junípero Serra Museum were opened to the public. Thousands of people thronged to the event carefully chosen to coincide with the 160th anniversary of Father Serra raising his rustic wooden cross on the hill below. Speeches were given, commemorative coins were distributed and a navy band played throughout the afternoon. For a brief period, Presidio Hill was acknowledged as the birthplace of Spanish San Diego. Some newspaper writers christened it the "Williamsburg of the West Coast."

Above: Aerial view of Presidio Hill, circa 1930. *Ray Brandes*.

Left: The buried adobe walls of Alta California's first mission on Presidio Hill, circa 1930. *Ray Brandes*.

While George Marston and his colleagues could be justifiably proud of the museum and the park, they knew there would never be the will or the funds to restore any of the presidio structures. When the fanfare was over, landscaping crews spread two to four feet of soil from the riverbed below over the adobe walls, filled the rooms with soil and created a series of mounds terracing down the hill. Once again, the site that had once been San Diego became a buried artifact of the past, its melted adobe walls just a part of the landscape.

Chapter 5

THE ARCHAEOLOGICAL RECORD

Uncloaking the Past

Some of the world's major cultural and archaeological sites were discovered by accident, including the famed caves at Lascaux, France. Others, such as the Great Pyramids of Egypt, seemed to have always been there awaiting excavation. On the United States East Coast, controversy still swirls around the exact location of Sir Walter Raleigh's Roanoke settlement and even portions of the far more successful settlement at Jamestown. In the case of the over 250-year-old San Diego Presidio, the exact location had been known for decades in 1965 when archaeologists turned their attention to the site. Ceremonies had been held there celebrating its founding, monuments had been set into the ground and postcards had touted the gently sloping hill as the birthplace of California. More attention was paid to an old palm tree at the foot of the hill. Although dubious, postcards and tourist leaflets claimed the venerable tree was planted by Junípero Serra himself. Occasionally, the local press would run a commemorative piece on the old fort or do a fashion photo shoot at the museum.

Presidio Hill is one feature of Presidio Park that is owned by the City of San Diego and managed by Parks and Recreation. With construction of the Junípero Serra Museum on the hill in 1929, the San Diego Historical Society (now the San Diego History Center) assumed operation of the museum. As San Diego approached its two-hundred-year anniversary in 1969, various civic events were proposed to mark the event. One of those events was to acknowledge the importance of the buried ruins.

To that end, in 1964, Dr. Raymond Brandes, newly appointed director of the San Diego Historical Society's Serra Museum, proposed an archaeological research and training program at the site. He recommended that a program then known as Historic Sites Archaeology be conducted on the ruins. San Diego State College (now San Diego State University) had an active and well-staffed Department of Anthropology and was promoted as the institution to conduct the study. The historical society would serve as the primary sponsor and act as a liaison with the city.

The proposed program had several objectives and sought to serve disparate masters, including architects, city officials, educators and civic interests. In the short term, leading up to the centennial year 1969, the focus was on educating and training students. Historic archaeology was in its infancy early in the 1960s, with few professional practitioners. The proposed excavations on Presidio Hill explored unfamiliar territory in the fields of archaeology and anthropology. Over the next decade, the excavations and research thoroughly documented the important place of Presidio Hill in Southern California and San Diego history. Secondarily, and probably always unlikely, just as it was in 1929, the feasibility of restoring at least some of the ruins would be explored. Artifacts from the ongoing excavations would be proudly displayed at the Serra Museum. For the first time, guided tours of the ruins and the excavations were offered to interested groups, including literally thousands of schoolkids.

The afternoon of Sunday, March 7, 1965, was in the high sixties, and an early morning sprinkle or two had dampened the grassy knoll shrouding the historic ruins. In a nod to the site being the first Catholic church in Alta California, the Most Reverend Bishop Francis J. Furey, apostolic administrator of the Diocese of San Diego, blessed the archaeological site. San Diego City Vice Mayor Ivor de Kirby, chair of the County Board of Supervisors Frank Gibson and San Diego Historical Society President Mrs. Lester L. Wittenberg broke ground not with shovels but with the tools of the archaeologists' trade—trowels. For the first time since the 1920s, the buried settlement would yield its secrets.

Basic surveying and mapping of the mounds associated with the subterranean buildings was conducted, and students then walked up the hill to the museum for a preliminary lecture. Dr. Brandes served as liaison for the historical society. Dr. Paul Ezell, San Diego State professor, who was on temporary leave in South America, agreed to direct the excavations. Ezell would resume control of the field school on his return the following year. Probably unknown to Ezell at the time, he would spend the next decade directing the excavations. With only sporadic exceptions, excavation at the site continued until the summer of 1976. While Dr. Ezell toiled at the site most Saturdays and on some weekdays, his wife, Greta Ezell, conducted most of the historical research, especially those materials in Spanish. His work in the field and her research on archival materials laid to rest old myths and misconceptions about the presidio and its people.

In the days before ground-penetrating radar (GPR) became a common field technique, buried ruins were opened based on sketchy maps such as those the San Diego Historical Society had and archaeological intuition. Limited excavation by Percy Broell in the late 1920s suggested the mounds were the remnants of troop living quarters or barracks. The only buried feature that seemed for certain was the mound under the imposing Panamanian-Serra Cross a little farther uphill. Everyone agreed that when the cross was erected in 1913, it was placed on the old commandant's home. What was in serious error was that the presidio church was assumed to be behind (east of) the commandant's house. As it turned out, several assumptions were substantially in error.

The general area selected for archaeological excavation comprised a long depression surrounded by gently rolling mounds about three feet high. Vegetation on the hill was generally sparse, and what existed around the edges of the ruins was dominated by nonnative ornamentals and a few pine trees. It was several years later that one of the pine trees on the western side of the excavation near the front entrance to the church had to be sacrificed in the name of science. Arborists and garden clubs cried foul, but science was served.

Following standard procedures, the study area was divided into smaller units for excavation and controlled measurements. The largest mound feature was labeled "A," the room next to it "B" and so on. At some point, the rooms were renumbered 1, 2 and so on up to at least number 8. Returning from his sabbatical in South America, Paul Ezell took over the direction of the site. He abandoned the concept of delineating the excavation by "rooms" and switched instead to control units five feet square excavated in six-inch levels. A central datum point that would guide all future measurements was established near what turned out to be the entrance to the baptistry. All excavation units from that point on had addresses that were east–west and north–south of that central data point. Using inches and feet in the sciences was fading, but this was before America embarked on a crusade to bring the metric system to even the liberal arts.

Most, but not all, soils were sifted through one-quarter-inch hardware cloth screens. Careful measurements of architectural elements, in situ (in place) artifacts and other features were made within each unit. Over time, the excavations revealed three main areas of artifact depositions: a large trash deposit in the courtyard, secondary trash deposited into what would have been the abandoned cemetery and secondary deposits within the abandoned chapel itself.

The upper levels just below the grass sod contained artifacts from the recent past. Picnickers, lovers and kids who used to slide down the icy mounds on cardboard sleds left their own detritus. Tokens for long-gone streetcars, silver 1950 dimes, bottle caps and other modern debris mark their passage. As the architecture of the buried walls and floors took shape, students with some degree of artistic talent were asked to provide scaled drawings. In addition to the scaled drawings, each student excavator was required to sketch the site in their lined composition notebook.

During the 1968 spring semester, San Diego City Mesa Junior College (now Community College) students under the supervision of Professor Michael Axford joined the crew. Overnight, the crew size swelled to over thirty excavators, including first-semester students, graduate students and volunteers. This relationship continued until the project closed out in 1976. Archaeology was gaining in popularity among students and vocationalists, so for the first time, San Diego State added a field class as a six-week summer session. In addition, Dr. Ezell was a big supporter of public archaeology and getting the layperson involved in the discipline. Against the advice of some of his academic colleagues, he accepted volunteers for the excavation. Over time, many of the volunteers worked their way from being just enthusiastic "bucket dumpers" to skilled excavators. Several achieved college degrees and went on to have careers in archaeology.

As the excavation uncovered more features, and despite assurances by old-timers and persons supposedly in the know, Dr. Ezell came to believe that the presidio chapel was not up the hill under the imposing brick Serra Cross but rather exactly where he was excavating. Even worse, as his crew cleared sizeable areas of a carefully laid tile floor (which turned out to be the chapel nave), they spotted areas where the tiles had slumped. Closer investigation led to the conclusion that the ladrillos in those areas had been removed, replaced and re-mortared. Then, over the decades, the soil settled and portions of the tile floor curved downward with it. Dr. Ezell knew from experience that the slumped rectangles were the location of human burials within the chapel.

As Dr. Ezell told this author later, the human burials beneath the chapel floor were the last thing in the world that he wanted to find. While some

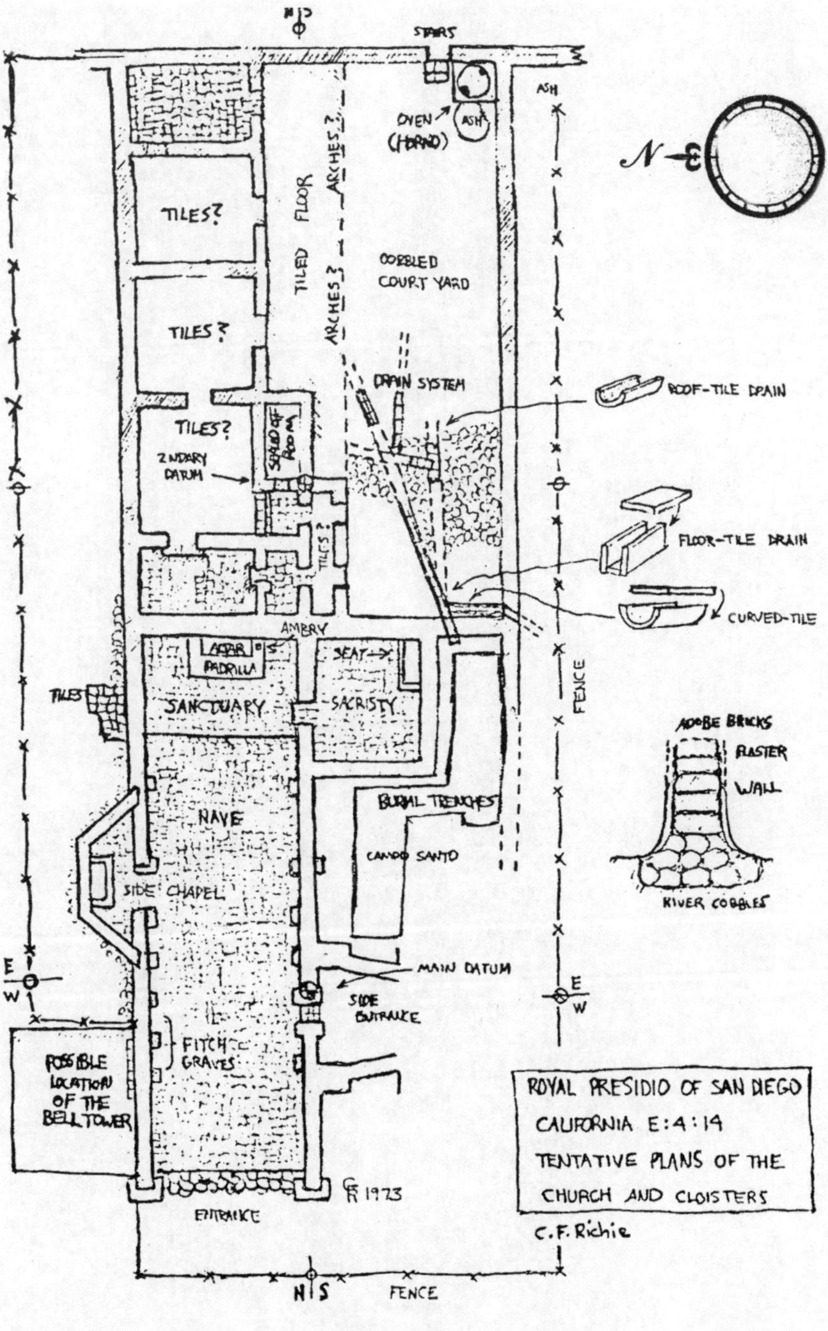

Scaled schematic map of presidio chapel excavations by C.F. Richie. *Author's collection.*

Burial beneath the tiled floor of the presidio chapel nave. *Author's collection.*

archaeologists may revel at the discovery of burials, Dr. Ezell knew the long hours it would take to excavate and analyze them, the potential religious and political implications and how the focus would be diverted from documenting the architecture and artifacts. In fact, there was virtually no way to avoid finding burials. They were under the chapel and baptistry floor, in the cemetery contiguous to the chapel and at sporadic locations throughout the site.

Dr. Ezell instructed his best excavators to carefully remove selected tiles and explore the subterranean pits. When excavation of these locations, most of which were in the front half of the nave, uncovered human remains, he instructed the crew to briefly record them, cover them with a thin layer of soil and excavate elsewhere. This led to a chaotic numbering system for more than one hundred burials.

Ezell, hoping to develop an official and formal policy for treatment of the remains, began consultation with the Catholic diocese, city officials and the historical society. Whether at that early stage Dr. Ezell knew that some of the burials were Native American or not is uncertain. Research on the presidio burial records had been minimal to this point. Regardless, in the late 1960s, it was rarely standard archaeological protocol to contact descendants of persons excavated in a consecrated cemetery, let alone potential Native American descendants.

As 1967 ended, the tally of recorded burials reached 20, and there were other "suspect" divots on the tile floor and nearby. Ultimately, there were at least 121 burials tabulated out of a known burial record from mission death records of over 220. The local press picked up the story of "mysterious graves," and visitors to the site swelled. To discourage the lookie-loos, tarps were kept over the burial pits and student tour guides were told to downplay the discoveries.

Dr. Ezell's worst fears of rising Native American involvement in the project occurred when Kumeyaay elder Rosalie Pinto Robertson and her brother Tony Pinto visited the site. The Pinto family was, and is, related to the ancient Hilmeup clan, and a María Hilmeup (spelled in the records as Cilmip) was the sixth burial recorded at the presidio in the 1770s. Her original record was reconstructed after the mission records were burned in the 1775 Tipai uprising. Probably unaware of that early burial, the Pintos seemed to believe that their descendant of concern had been buried much later. They accused Dr. Ezell of desecrating the graves of their ancestors and wanted the excavations stopped.

Removing and analyzing burials within the presidio chapel nave. Pictured to the right is Greta Ezell, historian and advisor. *Author's collection.*

According to retired anthropologist Dr. Jerome Levi, who was at the on-site meeting, the Pintos pointed out to Dr. Ezell where they believed their ancestor, possibly a grandmother, had been buried. Dr. Levi, following anthropological protocol, did not ask the Pintos the name of their ancestor or other details. Probing living Native people about the specifics of their ancestors was then, and often is now, a very sensitive subject.

In consultation with Catholic diocese officials and the City of San Diego, it was agreed to avoid the specific area of conflict but to continue the overall exploration. The position of the diocese was that persons buried in a consecrated Catholic cemetery were Catholics under the purview of the Church. In recent (2024) meetings with the Pinto family from the Jamul Indian Village, they revealed they are still disturbed by the excavation of the burials at the presidio and hope to discover more about their ancestor. Some uncertainty lingers as to when the ancestor was buried, whether the ancestor was actually excavated and, if so, whether the remains were ever removed from the ground. It was common practice, given the condition of many of the burials, to not remove them. Instead, osteological and forensic study was completed in the field.

Fully aware that many people do not have such concerns about the bones of the dead, in fact they seek them out, Dr. Ezell grew uneasy about the remains. He feared that what he called "cultish bone collectors" or grave robbers in search of gold would jump the chain-link fence, shovels in hand. After some shadowy figures were in fact seen lurking around the fences one evening, loyal students offered to camp on the site and serve as guards so Dr. Ezell could get some sleep and stay home in bed. As a side comment, twenty years later, when this author was excavating at the San Diego Mission, we had persons breaching the fence and searching for both bones and gold. They were dissuaded by a nine-millimeter Glock pistol.

From 1967 until the site was closed out in 1976, literally hundreds of students worked on the site, research papers were generated and at least a dozen of Dr. Ezell's students went on to long careers in teaching and professional archaeology. With no hope of long-term preservation or restoration, the decision was made to cover the adobe walls, which had continued to melt back into the soil, with plastic sheets and then place soil over the ruins. Later, the area was sodded and essentially returned to its 1965 status. For the second time in its history, the presidio ruins lay shrouded by dirt and grass. The collections from over eleven years of excavation and study remain at San Diego State University, where they are increasingly valued by non-Native scholars and local Kumeyaay persons. In some instances, human remains believed to be Native American have been returned to the tribes for repatriation and burial.

Throughout the 1970s, the buried presidio ruins were a tourist destination but also an educational opportunity for hundreds if not thousands of local schoolchildren. As part of the fourth-grade California history curriculum, students visited the site as well as going to Old Town. Programs run through extended adult education institutions also regularly held classes on the site. This author gave over sixty tours to all levels of interested students and visitors. The local National Public Broadcasting station (KPBS) filmed several episodes at the ruins as part of their San Diego History series.

As the university excavation gradually ran down, local television stations, including NBC, also filmed segments at the site, temporarily increasing public interest. No sooner had the San Diego State excavations closed out in September 1976 than Mesa Community College began their explorations. Led by Professor (later Dr.) Diane Barbolla, the focus of that program was to explore an area southwestward from the chapel complex. Based on early

Past director of the presidio excavations and author Richard Carrico giving a tour of the presidio site. *Author's collection.*

maps and descriptions, that area was believed to be the original gateway, prison and other military buildings.

The layout of the Mesa College excavation included ten excavation units. The first six were excavated in five-foot-square units using arbitrary six-inch levels. Heeding what appeared to be an American and scientific-based switch to metric, the last four units were excavated in ten-centimeter levels. In addition to discovering the original gateway and the prison, Barbolla's crew uncovered a treasure-trove of artifacts and faunal remains in a trash pit over ten feet in depth.

The Mesa College fieldwork concluded in 1985, although cataloging and artifact analysis continued until 1991. The analysis led to a significant thesis on the topic of faunal remains, a series of papers presented at professional conferences and publications in academic journals by Dr. Barbolla and others. Barbolla's doctoral dissertation focused on her findings from the excavations. Her overall conclusion was that her area of study had been occupied and used for over sixty years and served several military and domestic functions.

Beginning in September 1987 and extending until May 1990, Dr. Brad Bartel of San Diego State University conducted excavations on what he correctly termed the northern wing of the presidio. The northern wing was on the northern side of the parade ground, approximately one hundred yards from the chapel complex. This wing has always been assumed to be the living area for the troops, including small casitas for the married couples and other dwellings for the single men.

Craft workers and other nonmilitary personnel may have also lived there. Bartel's excavation of architectural features was limited, but he uncovered extensive trash pits. When he completed his excavation in 1990, the rooms and features were covered over and ultimately placed under a cover of mulch and bark. The collections from Dr. Bartel's work are housed at the San Diego State University Collections Management Department.

In 1993, Dr. Jack Williams, director of the Center for Spanish Colonial Archaeology and a well-known scholar of Spanish borderlands history, began an excavation close to the earlier work of Dr. Bartel. Williams's crew was made up of work program youths with minimal archaeological excavation experience. Despite that, under the guidance of Williams, between 1993 and 1997, his crew made significant discoveries.

Overall, Williams better defined the layout of the living quarters, conducted important research on the quantity and types of Mexican maiolicas (also spelled majolica) on the site and presented papers on the men and women who lived at the presidio. More than anyone else, Williams delved heavily into original primary Spanish records. This allowed him to tease out large and small details about the people who occupied the site. Dr. Williams passed away before he could complete his studies. His collections and records are being curated at the City of San Diego.

Archaeological excavations beginning informally in the mid-1920s and then professionally in the 1960s through 1990s removed literally tons of sod, fill dirt and debris. The archaeologists discovered entire rooms, floors, burials, drainage systems, trash pits and virtually every facet of Spanish and Californio life on the hill. The three professional excavations are referred to as the Chapel Excavations of Paul Ezell, the Gateway Excavations of Diane Barbolla and the North Wing Excavations of Bartel and Williams.

Chapter 6

THE ENGINEERING AND ARCHITECTURE OF THE PRESIDIO

Spanish Colonial Norms Meet La Frontera

Introduction

When first constructed, the various buildings, parade grounds and stables at the presidio were essentially terraced or cut into the sloping hillside. Some of the excavated soils from terracing were used as fill and to level out the landform to provide stable footing for the various buildings. Until the mission itself was moved farther up the valley in 1774, church officials and the military officers competed for resources, food supplies and laborers. Supply ships from mainland Mexico were unreliable, and the region lacked suitable stone to quarry for construction. In the early years, abandonment of the settlement on Presidio Hill was seriously considered.

Gradually, with various episodes of construction, adobe structures rose from the brown adobe soil. The architecture, style and construction materials of the presidio reflected the local environment and decades of adapting Spanish architecture to the varied lands of mainland Mexico and Baja California. By the mid-1750s, what arose in Nueva España (New Spain) came to be recognized as the Spanish Colonial style. The existing Mission San Diego de Alcalá, built in 1805 and virtually rebuilt in the 1930s, is a classic local example of Spanish Colonial style.

The terms "Spanish Colonial architecture" and "Spanish Revival" have been much used and abused over the years. Their original meaning described architecture from Iberia, specifically Spain, with strong Moorish elements that were then adapted to conditions and materials in the New World. Major

Mission San Diego de Alcalá. This reconstructed structure was originally built in 1805. *Author's collection.*

themes of style and construction include the use of stucco over adobe, curved tile roofs, graceful archways, low-pitched roofs and courtyards.

Even though the San Diego Presidio was not constructed as a town per se, the general Spanish concept of *la traza* layout was applied. La traza was a template used throughout Mexico proper and Baja and Alta California during the early and late colonial era. The layout of the presidio followed the traza by having a central plaza, in this case a parade ground. The plaza was surrounded by storerooms, a church, homes for the military and religious officials, corrals and stables. Given its role as a governmental hub, the presidio also housed a prison.

The northwestern portion of the presidio included barracks for the unmarried soldiers and casitas or small houses for the married soldiers and civilian craft workers. A large dwelling for the commandant sat near the top of the presidio in the central part of the fort. This structure would also be the quarters for visiting Mexican officials. From 1825 to 1831, it housed José Maria Echeandía, the governor of Alta California. At this time, San Diego became the de facto capital of Alta California. Lower on the hill at the edge of a cliff, there was the narrow gateway, guardhouse, storage areas, perhaps the armory and prison.

Bastions designed to hold small cannons were in the southeast and northwest corners. Corrals and stables were on the eastern side of the presidio uphill and downwind from the main presidio structures. Near the stables, but beyond the twenty-foot-tall adobe walls of the presidio, stood a *casa mata*. This building was a Spanish version of casement, a thick-walled enclosure for armaments. When the archaeological excavations began in 1965, this layout was not clearly understood. The chance discovery of what came to be known as the Mariano Guadalupe Vallejo Map by Professor Richard Whitehead in 1982 provided many of the details for the presidio. The Vallejo map augmented archaeological discoveries. Vallejo, an important figure in California history and the namesake of the Northern California town, was stationed at the presidio in 1824. At seventeen, he served as a cadet at the fort. His map, completed in the 1870s, was based on his recollections in the 1920s.

Prior to 1774, the colonial settlers' spiritual needs were served by the presidio's "church complex." The term pulls together the garrison's adobe

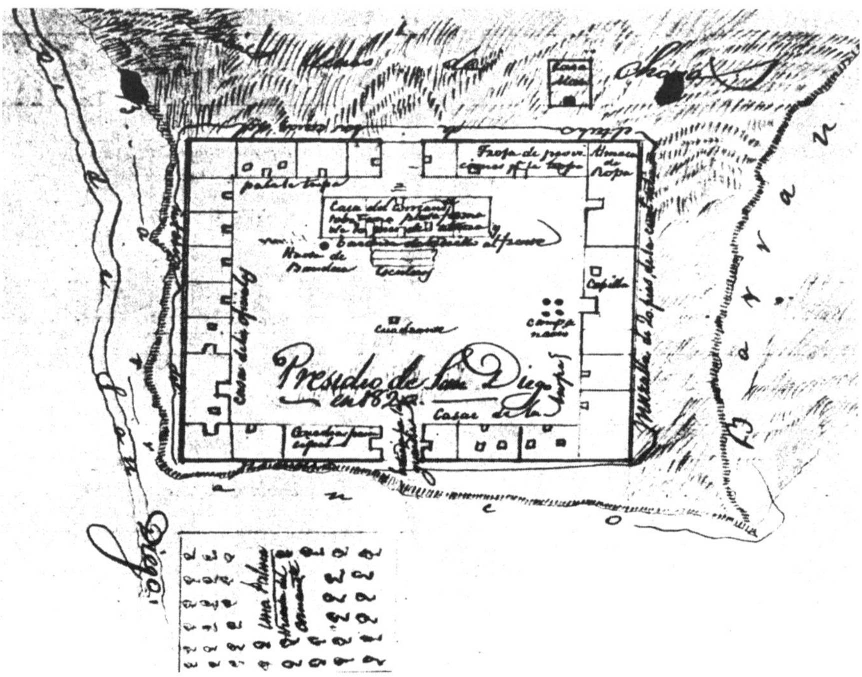

Mariano Vallejo's map of the San Diego Presidio, circa 1820, from his reminiscences of 1876. *Bancroft Library, Berkeley, California.*

chapel cemetery (aka campo santo), priest's quarters, church storage rooms (ancillary nonmilitary structures) and a courtyard. Non-consecrated open ground, where burials of the unconverted took place, might be viewed as set apart from the "church complex" designation, since it lacked any Roman Catholic imprimatur.

The San Diego Presidio served primarily as a military and secular institution rather than as a city per se. The layout of the presidio blended la traza with patterns established for earlier presidios in Mexico. This included a defensive wall that encompassed the facility, bastions housing cannons in two corners, a commandant's residence, barracks for the unmarried soldiers, an armory and residences for the married soldiers, craft workers and other civilians.

Chapel Excavation

The different Catholic orders (Franciscan, Dominican and Jesuit) brought their own stylistic expression to their colonial missions and chapels. Before its relocation upriver in 1774, the San Diego mission at the presidio did not follow the well-established pattern of placing the religious center within a Native village. Instead, as one element of the overall presidio, the mission building sat within the strategically placed fortification. In turn, the presidio itself was on an easy to defend hill overlooking San Diego Bay. While precontact Kumeyaay may have hunted or collected plants from the hill, their settlement, Kosaii, meaning "dry place" or "drying place," was near a spring just below the hill.

As the first Franciscan mission in Alta California, Mission San Diego de Alcalá began in 1769 on the hill as a hut and then as a simple adobe building with a thatched roof. Later, the most dominant structure within the church complex was the presidio's adobe chapel, which was begun in 1778 and completed in April 1783. It replaced earlier wooden structures and what was described in 1782 as a miserable hut used as a church. The 1780s structure included a long nave (approximately ninety feet and eighteen feet wide), a side chapel later cut into the original nave wall on the north, a baptistry on the southwest side of the nave and a sacristy on the south side of the nave. An altar and altar platform (*predella*) abutted the end (eastern wall) of the sanctuary.

Behind the altar, the east wall would have had a *retablo* with niches where statues of saints were displayed. Following Franciscan fervor for the Virgin

Architectural reconstruction of Zúñiga's 1783 chapel drawn by Randi Hawkins and Richard Carrico. *Author's collection.*

Mary, the San Diego Presidio chapel had a four-foot-tall, wooden and gesso (a type of plaster) statue of the Immaculate Conception either on the altar or set into the retablo. Other saints may have occupied niches in the adobe wall.

To the east of the nave was a series of rooms, including living quarters for the visiting priest, storerooms and other rooms with uncertain functions, although the room immediately behind the sanctuary may have served as a dressing room or ready room for the priests. These buildings were apparently laid out on magnetic north rather than true north, with an approximately 3.5-degree variance. That the early colonists possessed a compass with which to lay out lines is verified by the mission inventory.

To the south of the chapel and its contiguous rooms were two large open areas; one served as the cemetery, and to the east there was a courtyard that contained a *horno* (domed oven) for cooking and a drain system to carry water away from the buildings. On a slight slope, a cobble path or walkway extended to the southwest from the priest's quarters, storerooms and across the courtyard. Based on the drainage system and the silt encountered during excavation, the cobbled walk provided a path across what must have been at the time a muddy, slippery ground surface. This open area and an area south of the sacristy, especially in later years, also served as a repository for trash and refuse. These outdoor areas were, as with the rest of the presidio, surrounded by an adobe defense wall. To the left (north) of the chapel, entrance bells were hung from a wooden scaffold; a formal bell tower was never constructed.

Construction of Zúñiga's 1783 chapel followed basic engineering common to many Southern California Spanish structures. Given that a copy of Vitruvius's *The Ten Books of Architecture* was in the mission library, Zúñiga or one of his artisans may have used that guide to construct the chapel. As with most of the structural walls at the presidio, they were constructed of unfired adobe blocks that were set on slightly raised cobble foundations to reduce capillary water action and erosion of the blocks. The cobble foundations consisted of river cobbles that weighed between fifteen and fifty pounds. They were typically buried in a three-foot-deep and thirty- to forty-inch-wide trench. The cobble foundation rose approximately six inches above the ground surface, at which point the unfired adobe blocks were set into a matrix of sand or mortar. Stucco on both the interior and exterior would have reduced erosion of the adobe blocks but required constant maintenance and reapplication.

Typically, the unfired adobe blocks measured twelve inches by ten inches, although there was substantial variation. Floor tiles also came in various sizes. Some were square, measuring ten inches by ten inches; others were twenty-two inches by eleven inches; and still others were twenty inches by sixteen inches. The variation may reflect different periods of construction or aesthetics. For instance, the tiles in the baptistry and on the altar platform measured twelve inches by six inches, providing a more pleasing appearance in those areas. Curved fire clay roof tiles (*tejas*) also varied in size from nine inches wide and twelve inches to nine inches by twenty inches. The roof tiles were typically one-half inch thick and weighed approximately five pounds each. An enduring folklore suggests that the roof tiles were formed on the thighs of female Native workers.

The soil beneath the floors was first leveled and then most often layered in sand, then capped with fired clay floor tiles (*ladrillos*) joined by mortar. The artisans constructing the presidio buildings would have made Roman-type mortar by mixing fine sand, ash and lime made from ground and burned

Cobble foundations for unfired adobe block walls. *Author's collection.*

limestone or marine seashells. Kilns used to make the stucco have reportedly been located close to Mission (False) Bay.

In the early years, the chapel and other structures were roofed with thin beams and reed thatching. In later years, large wood beams formed the superstructure and were then covered in curved roof tiles. The source of large timbers was fifty miles east in Corte Madera Valley. Kumeyaay laborers with teams of oxen hauled the timbers to the presidio, where they were hewn and planed.

As noted, the interior adobe walls were plastered with a type of stucco made from crushed and burnt seashells and sand. Archaeological investigation in rooms behind the nave revealed that sometimes pieces or chunks of unreduced shell were used in the stucco whitewash. The shells were typically marine shells, common to the mudflats and the bay shore.

Sometimes, especially at the lower levels of the walls in the church, paintings or frescoes of vines or leaves were applied to the plaster. In some Spanish churches, the walls and columns were painted to give the appearance of gardens and trees. Symbolically, the gardens and trees evoked the Garden of Eden and humans' pastoral beginnings. The upper level of the nave walls just below the roof known as the clerestory was pierced by windows to allow light into the otherwise dark nave area. Upright wooden columns, called pilasters, which sat on bases formed from adobe tiles, were painted to produce a faux marble effect. In other mission churches, these pilasters were stone or stacked and plastered adobe tiles. Throughout California, environmental factors such as the presence or absence of stone and timber determined the construction materials.

Excavation of the column bases that fronted the baptistry revealed traces of blue pigment or paint that may have bled off from the columns. This occurrence was also noted by Percy Broell when his team excavated that area in the 1930s. Some of the pilaster bases themselves were inscribed with cross hatches. The altar rail was wrapped in a copper sheathing, portions of which were excavated during archaeological investigations.

The altar itself was made of stacked adobe tiles of varying sizes about five feet in height, covered with stucco and then embellished with a sacramental cloth covering. Contemporary accounts describe a silk rug in front of the altar. To the right of the collapsed altar, excavation uncovered the sacrarium, which is a drain on which a basin (*piscina*) sat. This device was used to dispose of spoiled or unused sacramental wine and to wash sacramental vessels. This feature reflects the Catholic Church's strict rules for disposal of sacred items. At the time of its discovery, it was mistakenly

Stucco plaster with colored designs applied to adobe wall in presidio chapel nave area. *Author's collection.*

This page, top: Incised cross hatching on pilaster column base. *Author's collection.*

This page, bottom: Chapel altar constructed of fired adobe tiles. *Author's collection.*

Opposite, top: Sacrarium in altar floor used to dispose of unused sacramental wine and host. *Author's collection.*

This page, bottom: Overhead photograph of priest's room behind (east of) the chapel altar. *Author's collection*.

Opposite, top: Presidio church side chapel and nave, looking east. *Author's collection.*

Opposite, bottom: Nuestra Señora del Carmen, Orizaba, Veracruz. Note scallop shell above entrance. *Robert Jackson.*

This page, top: Entrance to chapel baptistry. Note the pilaster column bases in the foreground. These supported the doorway with the scallop casting. *Author's collection.*

This page, bottom: The curved chapel baptistry with missing tiles beneath which a burial was uncovered. *Author's collection.*

called the ambry. The ambry would have been a wooden cabinet fitted into the nave wall or a niche in the wall. It was used to store vessels and sacramental clothing.

Directly behind (northeast of) the nave and the altar, archaeologists discovered the priest's quarters and a storeroom. The priest's room would have been used only occasionally, given that after 1776, the priests were housed at the mission. In addition to the chapel nave and sacristy themselves, the San Diego mission had a curved baptistry on the right side of the nave and a small side chapel on the left side. As discussed within the narrative regarding burials, the side chapel contained three of the more interesting graves.

The baptistry, located on the right (southern) side of the chapel, at one time contained a large stone baptism font. This font was reportedly taken to the newly completed San Diego mission in 1774. As excavation continued at the entrance to the baptistry, a nearly intact fallen doorway was encountered on the chapel floor. The wall and its arched top were carefully excavated and revealed a traditional scallop shell design. Doorways with scallop designs above them symbolize the pilgrimage of the apostle James, as well as rebirth and protection. Such artistic and architectural symbolism can be found all over Mexico and Catholic Europe. In Christian tradition, James's body returned home, floating on a single large scallop shell. Excavation within the baptistry itself revealed a burial underneath the adobe tile floor.

Gateway Excavation

Downslope and to the west of the chapel and across what may have been an open field lay the gateway, the prison, probably an armory and other military structures. The prison was described as made up of rooms that may have varied from six feet by six feet to as large as ten feet by ten feet. The cells, which one Native American likened to a barred cage, were dark and dank. A partial excavation of a cell floor revealed that the subfloor consisted of several levels of large (one-foot to one-and-a-half-foot diameter) boulders layered on each other. This may have deterred inmates from attempting to escape by digging through the floor. Evidence for the gateway, which was not situated in its present location, was just a gap in the western defense wall.

Perhaps the most surprising discovery from Dr. Barbolla's gateway exploration was encountering a massive trash pit. On the western edge of the presidio on a steep bluff, the trash pit may have been associated with the troop housing and general population rather than the chapel complex. The pit, which extended almost fifteen feet below the current ground surface, produced thousands of artifacts, the bulk of which were local Tizon brown ware sherds and Maiolica ware produced in mainland Mexico. Fragments of roof tiles and floor tiles were also recovered.

Crucifixes, buttons, animal bone, shellfish and Indigenous stone tools were recovered from the excavation. An extensive analysis of the faunal remains showed that butchered and other food waste was repeatedly dumped in this area. This collection has been catalogued, and academic papers have been published on topics such as the Maiolica and faunal remains, but overall, the collection still offers tremendous research potential.

The North Wing Barracks and Housing Excavations

Like the Gateway Excavation, archaeological testing by Dr. Bartel and Dr. Williams produced significant information regarding the layout of the troops' quarters and the living areas separate from the chapel. The information from these excavations has been only sparsely disseminated, although it will be available for researchers in the future.

The picture that has emerged from the field notes is that the north wing contained small casitas for the married troops and barracks for the single men. At least one U-shaped adobe structure may have been a common food storage area. An engineering detail rarely seen in the Chapel Excavations, several of the tile floors were underlain by cobbles. This was no doubt an effort to level and stabilize the floor on the sloping ground surfaces.

Because Dr. Bartel's excavation was only exploratory, his excavation units did not encompass any singular room or structure that would better define their function or size. While the units produced large amounts of faunal remains, Tizon brown ware pottery, Maiolica ceramics and floor/roof tile, accurate quantification is not available. One important facet of the excavation was that Tizon brown ware occurred substantially more often than the Mexican or European wares. This may be sound evidence that Kumeyaay women were making or procuring pottery for use at the presidio. They and other presidial wives were likely making use of brown ware as their daily utilitarian cooking, storage and tableware.

The Williams excavation at the north wing is equally problematic at this point. A preliminary catalogue has been prepared, but the information is not readily available in a useable format. Based on generalized notes and

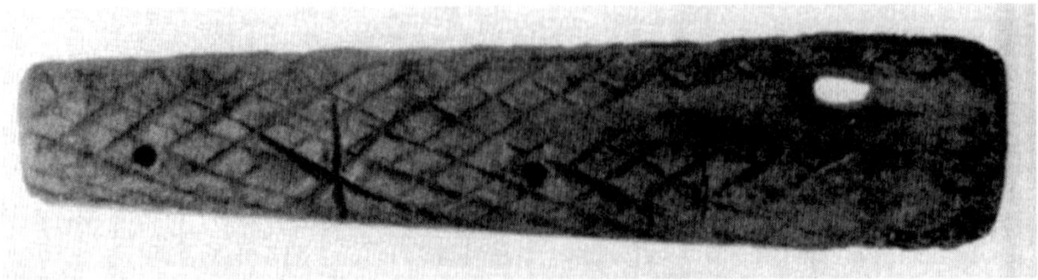

Incised bone handle from Bartel's north Gateway Excavation. *San Diego State University Collections Management.*

information available during the excavations, Dr. Williams uncovered and analyzed entire rooms and features within the wing. He concluded that many of the rooms had stamped dirt floors, while others had tile floors. This may have been a difference between the officers' quarters (if they were situated there) and the enlisted men's housing. Williams concurred with Bartel that some of the dwellings may have been at least partially destroyed by a fire in the early years of occupation. This may have taken place when reeds and brush were used for roofing prior to fired clay tiles being installed.

In those areas assumed to be used for cooking, both archaeologists found milling tools (manos, pestles and metates), food refuse with a predominance of immature cow bone (less than two years), chicken bone, fish bone and shellfish. At least one small *horno* or *estufa* (stove/oven) was discovered with a telltale layer of fine ash in front of the fire door. One of the more interesting finds reported by Bartel was an incised bone utensil handle. Whether the cross-hatched incisions were decorative or for gripping purposes is uncertain. Dr. Bartel also discovered the blacksmith area, as evidenced by metal slag, forged metal fragments and bent mule shoes and horseshoes. The amount of slag and melted metal strongly suggested that a foundry of some sort stood on the site. A blacksmith, such as Felipe Romero, was a highly regarded person in frontier communities. On the frontier, utilitarian objects were manufactured and repaired out of necessity. Romero, or another blacksmith, may have made the rustic artisan-appearing metal crucifixes and Christ figures discovered on the site.

Chapter 7

OVERVIEW OF THE POPULATION OF THE PRESIDIO

By the time the Spanish military and Franciscan missionaries moved north from Baja California and northern Mexico into Southern California, they were an ethnic population vastly different from the Spaniards who settled early colonial Mexico. Most Southern California settlers in the mid- to late 1700s were a combination of mixed blood. This mixture reflected European heritage, persons of Spanish and Native Indigenous blood (frequently labeled as Mestizo) and a blend of Indigenous/Spanish and Afro-Caribbean labeled as mulatto (a term in disfavor over the past few decades). This ethnic mixture was especially true of the enlisted soldiers and laborers.

At the point of their arrival in 1769 and in the following decades, the people of the presidio were well on their way to being more Californio than Spaniard. What is meant by "Californio" is that they were less engaged with mainland Mexico and governmental forces in Mexico City. They were less bound by staid Spanish traditions and by the Catholic Church. Exceptions to this were the twenty-five or so Catalonian volunteers who initially hailed from Spain. As was common on the frontiers of both Californias, the mixed-ethnicity colonists also gradually adopted at least some Indigenous traits, language and foods. Frontier settlements throughout the world historically experience this blending of cultures.

The early settlers in Alta California were often referred to as *norteños* (people of the north), an acknowledgement of the geographic separation. This label set them off from the Spaniards and, later, Mexicanos to the south. Yet even though they were ethnically diverse, they shared common cultural experiences and bonds. They were Catholic; swore at least feigned allegiance to the Spanish king (in the years before 1821); ate a diet based on corn, flour, beans and tortillas; and valued similar societal norms. The soldiers and officers were expected to carry on the centuries-old military traditions that were codified in no uncertain terms. But through the decades, this commonality faded.

The non-Indigenous composition of the presidio varied by number, gender and ethnicity over the decades. A census taken in 1790 reflected the male adult population and an emphasis on military forces. In 1775, Lieutenant José de Zúñiga commanded the forces supported by an *alferez* (captain), five noncommissioned officers, forty-six enlisted men, a blacksmith and a carpenter. One soldier was listed as a deserter imprisoned in the presidial prison. The blacksmith and carpenter were married, as were thirty-five of the fifty-three soldiers. The presence of wives and families signaled an increase in the domestic nature of the facility. In many ways, the once sparsely populated presidio was becoming a village, a frontier settlement. Perhaps surprisingly, ninety-four children composed the largest population at the presidio, almost a 2:1 ratio.

Of the fifty-six males at the presidio in 1790, more than one-half of whom were married, 55 percent self-identified as *Español* or *Españole*. The next largest group (16 percent) identified as *color quebrado*, which was a somewhat ambiguous term applied unevenly to persons of African ethnicity mixed with Español, mestizo or even mulatto. Almost 11 percent were Afro-Caribbean, a blend of African and Caribbean native called at the time mulatto. These three groups composed 83 percent of the adult male population, followed by smaller populations of mestizo, Indio, Coyote and people born in Europe (only three). The wives of the soldiers and artisans were also diverse.

Besides their ethnicity, the origins of the presidial population were equally diverse. While general histories call the presidio population and their culture Spanish, that nomenclature is too broad. Thirty-seven geographic locales and regions were represented at the presidio, including single examples from Belgium, Aragon and Cuba. The colonists' "Spanishness" was more ascribed than real, more defined by their governmental allegiance than ethnicity.

The largest population group, which includes soldiers, settlers and their wives, was from Villa Sinaloa, over nine hundred miles southeast on the western coast of mainland Mexico, followed by Loreto Baja California, over seven hundred miles south. In contrast to most of the Hispanic women and men, the Native Indigenous women hailed from closer areas. This included the San Diego region, the Colorado River area to the east and Baja

California to the south. Those from the San Diego region included local villagers (La Punta, Otai, Jacum and Jelleagua), as well as two Natives from the Rio Colorado/Yuma area in what is now western Arizona. La Punta and Otai were in the South Bay, Jacum in the mountains southeast of the presidio and Jelleagua near present-day Del Mar.

One woman, a mestizo named María Matilde Berdugo (Verdugo), called Mission Santa Clara in Northern Baja California home before taking up residence in San Diego. Native women from Baja California included a Tipai widow, a married woman from Mission San Miguel and a Cochimi from Mission San Gertrudis.

Only one person identified in the 1790 census was native to San Diego. That was a young Indigenous woman, Sinusin, who married a Spanish soldier. She hailed from the South Bay region of San Diego. In later years, other Native and mestizo wives would join Sinusin at the presidio, forming the backbone of the domestic scene. Given this mix of origins and ethnicity, it is easy to see that San Diego has always been an ethnically diverse region.

The non-European population at the presidio (the Indigenous people of Alta and Baja California and mainland Mexico) waxed and waned over the decades, just as the Spanish/Californio population did. Because the Native people rarely appear, except as a grouping in the census data or padrons, their presence must be teased from baptismal, marriage and death records. We know that less than a decade before the presidio was abandoned in 1835, a census/inventory of Native people at the presidio listed twenty-eight men, twenty-two women and ten children. These 60 Native people were an integral part of the presidial population.

The Native person who we know the most about is Sinusin, a young Tipai woman from the South Bay region of San Diego. In approximately 1764, five years before the founding of Mission San Diego at the presidio, a female child, Sinusin, was born to Malac and Talta, a Tipai couple living at Apusquele at the southern end of San Diego Bay. Apusquele was a large village near present-day Bonita and extending to the coast. Situated along El Camino Real (the Royal Road or King's Road), a major dirt trail that linked lower and upper California, Apusquele became an important Christian village. When Malac, Sinusin's father, took Catholic baptism in 1774, he took the name Benito, and his wife became Tecla. Sinusin took the rites on the same day and became Clara.

In 1779, at age fifteen, Sinusin (Clara) married Josef Antonio Leyva (Leyba), a presidial soldier. They lived at the presidio, where a small casita would have been assigned to the two of them. Over the next twelve years,

Petra, a young Paipai woman from Santa Catarina, Baja California. *John P. Harrington Papers, National Anthropological Archives.*

Clara had at least one son and five daughters. On her children's baptismal records, they are noted as mestizo. Three of these children died before 1792, and only one outlived her. At least one child and possibly two are buried at the presidio.

From her traditional South Bay Tipai village, Sinusin grew to maturity among presidial women from Northwest Mexico, Baja California and Alta California. Daily, Sinusin would have heard Spanish dialects from Mexico, Baja California, Cuba and Catalonia, as well as native Cochimi speakers from Baja California.

Clara's first husband, Josef Antonio, a *soldado cuero* (leather jacket) soldier, was apparently murdered at an unnamed Kumeyaay village sometime around 1788. She subsequently married José Manuel Bustamante, an Afro-Caribbean presidial soldier from Cuba. Her new husband is just one example of the multi-ethnic composition of the presidial community.

In the 1790 census, Clara and José are listed as having four children, three from her previous marriage and Marta, a newborn by José. They would have another daughter, Josefa Clara. Two years later, a daughter, Maria de Jesus, age twelve, died and was buried at Mission San Juan Capistrano. This shows that Clara and José had probably moved there by 1792.

On March 20, 1806, Sinusin Clara Leyva Bustamante died at San Juan Capistrano and is buried there in the mission cemetery. She was forty-two years old. In her lifetime, Sinusin witnessed the arrival of Spanish colonists, saw the construction and then razing of Mission San Diego, experienced daily life at the presidio and then at Mission San Juan Capistrano, wed two soldiers of varying ethnicity, birthed seven daughters and one son and buried at least five of them. One of her daughters later lived in an adobe in the Pueblo de San Diego, now Old Town San Diego.

By the time of her death, Sinusin carried an unusual title—ethnically, she was listed as "India" on her death record, but in a side note penned by the priest, she was also listed as "Razon," a person of reason bridging two worlds. She was truly a *Mujer de Presidio* and, perhaps more importantly, a *Mujer del Mundo*, a woman of the world.

Unlike for Sinusin, we have only fragments of information about the other Native persons living at the presidio. Only one Native woman, Anna

Mariá, married to a non-Native, a soldier, José Lobo, is listed as buried at the presidio. Her home at the time of death is listed as the presidio. Anna Mariá would have been one of the presidial wives who lived and ran a household in the troop casitas. She died in 1797, and there is apparently no record of her baptism or her marriage.

Fabian, a Cochimi from a Native village near Mission San Fernando de Velicatá, came north with Lieutenant Jose de Zúñiga in 1781. The mission near his native village in Baja California had been founded by Father Junípero Serra in 1769. When Fabian arrived in San Diego with Zúñiga, he had already been baptized, perhaps by Father Serra on his brief stay there before coming to San Diego.

Fabian served as Lieutenant Zúñiga's personal valet from at least their arrival in San Diego in 1781 until his death in January 1789. He apparently never married. In his burial record, the priest, Juan Mariner, noted that Fabian was given full last rites and buried within the presidio chapel. Fabian is the only Native person for whom the burial record clearly states that he was buried in the church rather than listed as no location given or in the cemetery.

One of the functions of the presidio was to house people suspected of crimes or convicted of criminal activity. Because of records regarding *presidiarios* (prisoners), we know a little about several Indian prisoners who died while in captivity. These men were apparently buried at the presidio, including Naguasajo, an unconverted Tipai rebel leader from the village of Ha Kunyematt (El Corral) who hanged himself in his prison cell in August 1776. Prior to his suicide, Naguasajo received a visit from Father Serra, who begged the rebel to pray for atonement and conversion. Serra knew Naguasajo was one of the leaders of the first attack on the newly arrived colonists in 1769 but hoped for the rebel's salvation. Naguasajo remained steadfastly unrepentant and is unlikely to be buried in consecrated ground.

Tabaco, an alleged Iipai rebel leader from the distant village of Pa'mu (Pamo) near the present-day town of Ramona, had been taken hostage along with other leaders and brought to the presidio. Tabaco died of an unknown cause in his cell following intense interrogation by Commandant Rivera y Moncada. The other leaders were later released, although previous researchers erroneously declared that they had been executed. In fact, one or two accounts called the executions (which did not happen) the first public executions in California.

Four Kumeyaay men who were executed at the site between 1813 and 1826 are buried at the presidio. These men—Anciento from Apta (San

Bernardo near Poway), Tiburcio (Malquam) Cuilp from the ranchería of Qamatar (Hamatar location uncertain), Juan Bautista Guaycupuchal from the ranchería of Guamasui (Huamasuy location uncertain) and Vicente Meyapapuchal from Hapacuach near Santa Ysabel (present-day Santa Ysabel Reservation)—were all executed by musket fire. One of these unfortunate men may have been archaeologically discovered with a musket ball lodged in his throat region. Except for Meyapapuchal, who had led an attack on soldiers at the Asistencia (sub-mission) Santa Ysabel in the eastern mountains, the crimes that led to their executions were not stated. All four men received last rites prior to execution and are buried in consecrated ground near the chapel.

A Kumeyaay man, Juan Nepomuceno, died in the presidio prison of unknown causes and was buried in the chapel cemetery in 1778. Naltipoco, a Tipai from U'tai (Otay or Otai) who was imprisoned for unknown reasons, also died in his cell. A Gabrieliño or Tongva, Juan de Mata from Mission San Gabriel near present-day Los Angeles, who was killed during transport to an uncertain location, was also buried at the presidio. Miguel, another Gabrieliño, died in the presidio prison and received last rites and was buried tin the cemetery in 1818.

Other Native adults who appear in the burial records include persons from Apusquele (Sinusin's home), Mission Santa Gertrudis in Baja California, two persons other than Fabian from San Fernando de Velicata, an adult sailor from San Xavier in Baja California, a person from the South Bay Tipay village of Xaatt (Las Chollas), a person from Mission Santa Clara in Northern California and a person from Mission Santa Barbara.

Several Native children, some of whom were apparently living at the mission or "claimed" by the mission, and others living at the presidio, died and were buried at the presidio. Although they were listed as attached to the mission, assumedly their parents or godparents lived or worked at the presidio. In addition to one or two of Sinusin's daughters, these child burials include a two-month-old baby from the Tipay South Bay village of La Punta and a one-and-a-half-year-old child from Chewaayp (Santa Domingo) near present-day Tijuana.

Much later, decades after abandonment, perhaps reflecting the continuing sacredness of the place, at least four Native women were buried with traditional rites at the presidio between 1873 and 1875. One of these may have been a member of the Hilmeup clan of Kumeyaay and an ancestor to present-day Pinto family members. Newspaper accounts of the time reported that the women were sorrowfully mourned. In 1875, José, a well-liked Native tracker from what is now Old Town San Diego, was buried on Presidio Hill, complete with a funeral procession from Old Town and traditional mourning songs at his burial.

An overview of the Native people who appear in censuses and are buried at the presidio reveals their diversity. While today, Kumeyaay leaders may claim repatriation rights for Native remains from the presidio, at least four, possibly more, tribes are represented. Geographic homeland for the Native people includes San Diego County, Santa Barbara, San Gabriel, northern Baja California and mainland Mexico. This diversity parallels a similar variation in tribal membership and place of origin at Mission San Diego.

Chapter 8

THE ETHNIC COMPOSITION OF PEOPLE AT THE PRESIDIO

How to categorize the varied ethnic and racial "types" who lived on the frontier and at the presidio has already been touched on. Even contemporary observers were in a quandary, as shown by a response to an 1813 questionnaire inquiring about castes and castas in California. The response from Mission Santa Barbara said in part that determining the castes or the ethnicity of a person was virtually impossible. The same could certainly be said for San Diego and probably most of the upper California missions.

As used in this book, "españoles," "Spanish" and "gente de razon" refer to those occupants of the presidio who either self-identified as such or appear in mission records as such. In general, these three terms refer to persons of non-Indigenous origins who professed ties to Spain or, more broadly by the 1700s, to Mexico. Persons not within these categories were Indio, mestizo and quebrado/mulatto.

Based on the Spanish/Mexican Catholic mission burial records of the 213 persons recorded as buried at the cemetery and chapel, adults of several ethnicities formed the largest category. These adults composed 122 individuals, or 57 percent. Sub-adult, infant and child burials of all ethnicities comprised the remaining 43 percent of the total.

This relatively high percent for sub-adults reflects the sheer number of Españoles and Indigenous/mestizo children who lived at the garrison. The 43 percent may also reflect what may have been a high childhood mortality rate. Male non-Indian adults composed 55 percent of the overall adult population.

The slightly higher percentage of adult males (55 percent) versus female would be expected, given that the presidio was a military garrison, a facility with a marginally predominant male population. According to the mission records, forty-three of the burials were adult Natives, and twenty-nine of these were male. The higher percentage (67) of male versus female adult Natives would be expected, assuming not many Native adult males had wives at the presidio.

The fourteen female adult Indians were almost entirely wives of Spanish and Mexican soldiers and, less frequently, workers and widows. In addition, American period historic accounts noted that between 1873 and 1875, at least four "Indian women," presumedly indigents or workers/servants from the Pueblo de San Diego, were buried in the old presidio cemetery. These four women were, however, not recorded in the official church records.

The ethnic character of the presidio deceased reflects the varied cultural and ethnic diversity officially recorded for early colonial San Diego. Analysis of *padrones* (contemporary registers) noted that in 1782, about six in ten (60 percent) of the presidio population listed themselves as Españoles, persons of self-described Spanish ancestry (nearly all born in the Americas); 33 percent were mestizos (mixed Spanish and Indian blood); slightly less than 2 percent were of African/Spanish descent (Afro-Caribbean); a little less than 4 percent were grouped as simply "racially mixed"; and almost 2 percent were Indios. The total is slightly greater than 100 percent because of rounding. Eight years later, reflecting continued ethnic and racial mixing, persons at the presidio self-described as Españoles composed 52 percent, an 8 percent drop in that category. Racially mixed climbed to a little over 33 percent, followed by "Indios" at almost 9.5 percent.

Generally, the non-mestizo Native people buried at the presidio were local Kumeyaay or Cochimi from Baja California, while other members of the Indigenous population were often mixed (mestizos) from the interior of Mexico, Baja California and the San Gabriel/San Juan Capistrano or Santa Barbara missions north of San Diego. Kumeyaay people buried at the presidio in the Spanish/Mexican period came from a wide range of villages throughout the San Diego region, reflecting the success of conversion at many villages but failure to convert Kumeyaay at many others.

The Native villages most represented in the death and burial records were those closest to the presidio, including Ystagua, Apusquele and Rincon de Jamo, as well as more distant settlements including U'tay (Otay), Jacum (Jacumba) and Ahti (Las Chollas). Clan names were rarely entered for the presidio burials, but the Hilmeup, Escaripa and Quilp clans are represented.

Indians from the missions of Baja California included Natives from Mission San Ignacio, Mission Santa Gertrudis, Mission San Fernando de Velicatá, Mission San Xavier and Mission San Miguel. All of these Native people from Baja California were likely Cochimí from the interior region except for Tipai/Kumeyaay from nearby San Miguel. The unidentified Native women and José, who were buried on the hill in 1870s, cannot be affiliated with specific villages.

Chapter 9

MORTALITY DATA AND PHYSIOLOGICAL INFORMATION

The mission death records typically provide only minimal information about the cause of death at the presidio and the mission. Frequently, they offer little more than the name, gender and sometimes age. For children, parents are often noted; for adults, the name of the spouse, if applicable, is provided. Although literally thousands of people were buried at the nearby mission (the vast majority Native persons), fewer than 220 were buried at the presidio. This is, of course, a function of the much larger Native presence at the mission and possibly the living conditions there, i.e. a potentially higher death rate.

Overall, San Diego, both the mission and presidio, suffered lower mortality rates than most of Alta California's Spanish settlements. Except for the years 1810–14 and 1825–29, San Diego death rates for the predominantly Native population were consistently well below death rates of those for the combined other missions. Although many factors may have been at play, the primary reason was that Natives were not held in large numbers at the mission. The food insecurity at the San Diego mission coupled with the recalcitrant nature of the Kumeyaay stifled the missionaries' attempts to house larger numbers of converts. At San Diego at least, being baptized did not necessarily mean that a Native was "converted" and regularly attended mass.

Comparison of Death Rate Per Thousand, San Diego versus California

Period	San Diego	California	Difference
1785–89	65	91	-26
1790–94	55	79	-24
1795–99	57	88	-31
1800–04	48	98	-50
1805–09	65	91	-26
1810–14	71	73	-02
1815–19	67	81	-14
1820–24	61	73	-12
1825–29	74	75	-01
1830–34	62	50	+12
Mean Death Rate	56	78	

Death, however, by nontraditional diseases did occur in San Diego. San Diego was hit by epidemic diseases (measles and perhaps smallpox) in the 1806–08 period and again in the mid-1820s. The 1826–27 measles epidemic appears to be reflected in the overall death rate for those years. The Native population, given their lack of immunity and especially those living in crowded conditions at the mission, were hard hit by these epidemics.

Even as a small sample size, forensic data from the burials helps in filling in the gaps in our knowledge of life and death at the presidio. Overall, archaeological forensic data from analysis of almost one hundred burials combined with written records show that the causes of death included childbirth, execution by musket ball, hanging (suicide), arrowhead wounds and varied diseases (e.g., pneumonia). Most often, the cause of death may not have been known and was not stated.

Physiological analyses on ninety-one of the burials offer, for the first time, an overview of the health and living conditions of the people at the presidio. Arthritis was common among many of the occupants of the presidio, especially the elderly. Some of the individuals experienced anemia and/or osteoporosis. When compared with a small sample size for the mission, however, anemia occurred less often at the presidio. Also, when it did occur, the severity of anemia appeared to be less at the presidio. Similarly, hypoplasia (poorly formed tooth enamel), while present at the presidio, was again less common and less severe than at the mission. Hypoplasia is one indicator of nutrient-poor diet or insufficient diet. In general, it would appear that the mixed-ethnicity presidio population had more access to nutritious food than the Native population at the missions did.

Several male individuals at the presidio had bowed fibula (were bow-legged), possibly showing habitual horse riding. Besides horse-mounted soldiers, several vaqueros were assigned to the presidio. Both the mission and the presidio maintained herds of cattle and sheep requiring mounted herdsmen. Soldiers were also expected to occasionally make the long rides to other missions.

A pathological forensic analysis was conducted by graduate student Jeffrey Howard on ninety-one of the burials (78 percent of the total) that had been excavated at the time of his research. What follows is a brief discussion of the more outstanding pathologies and health issues noted by Howard in his thesis.

Howard discovered that at least one individual (Burial 2) had lesions on the ectocranial (exterior of the cranium) surfaces of his frontal and parietal bones, as well as abnormally formed femurs (thigh bones) exhibiting differential torsion and arthritic lumbar vertebrae and scapulae. He was a short man at about five feet, three inches and died between the ages of forty and fifty. Burial 40, a male older than forty-five years of age, exhibited increased thickness of bone and a lesion on his left maxilla. Burial 80, a male over forty-five years of age, had anemia and osteoporotic bone lesions. Number 81, a female between twenty-five and thirty-five years of age, suffered trauma to her right tibia and left fibula. Burial 83, a male, approximately thirty years old, who suffered from periodontal disease (see below), also exhibited osteoporosis.

Burial 28, an adult male, apparently suffered from congenital syphilis, only the second documented example in San Diego, the other being a Native child at Mission San Diego de Alcalá. This small number of examples of syphilis is based on a low sample—fewer than ninety-one individuals at the presidio and fewer than fifty from the mission. It is by no means a measure of the incidence of syphilis in the community. While perhaps exaggerated, some contemporary accounts imply that syphilis was common among some portions of the military and Native community. This condition was noted especially in the waning years of the Mexican period.

Jack Williams has suggested that some level of prostitution—often a source of syphilis—was occurring at the presidio, although he did not offer substantive evidence of that. There were, however, isolated instances of soldiers trading cloth, beads and other goods for sexual intimacy. Rape of Native women may have also contributed to the spread of the disease.

As one might expect within a population that lived between 1770 and 1850, the average height of the adults for which we have accurate data (sixteen individuals, or only 13 percent of those excavated) was significantly less than current populations. The non-Indian male average was five feet, five inches, and the female was five feet, four inches. The tallest male stood about five feet, seven inches, and the tallest female was about five feet, six inches. For the non-Indian population, these heights are well within the norm for Hispanic and non-Nordic populations at the time. For the Native population, the average male was five feet, four inches. The one measurable female Indian stood five feet, five inches.

The dentition of the study group varied. Dental caries were common, and several individuals suffered from infections and periodontal disease. Adult tooth loss was noted on several of the skulls, with Burial 63 (a female between forty and fifty years of age) having lost most of her teeth prior to death. Burial 83, a male between the ages of twenty and thirty, suffered dental abscesses and severe tooth loss. Those adults assumed to be Native people had greater wear on their molars, probably showing a diet dominated by ingestion of food with grit. Such grit or small particles of stone is common in cultures where corn, wheat and acorns are milled on stone metates.

The mortality rate and age of death for the occupants of the presidio are not clearly known, although given that most of the men were in the military and several married females a decade younger, the occupants may have been younger than a general village or pueblo population of the time. Older soldiers and artisans and their wives may have retired to other settlements and were not part of this study. Movement away from the presidio after establishment of the San Diego pueblo in 1820 may have siphoned off portions of the older, more well-established population.

It was a common practice of the time for Hispanic men to delay marriage until they were better able to support a family. In the presidio's case, soldiers might seek attaining a higher rank before marriage. By contrast, young women were expected to enter marriage at least by their mid- to late teens. Of the burials observed for which age could be determined, ten persons were estimated to have died before the age of eighteen.

This forensic data is consistent with a review of the mission death records, which previously showed that between 1780 and 1831, thirty-eight children, ranging in age from one day to eleven years, were buried at the presidio. For the adult population, it is likely that most individuals living and dying at the presidio died in their mid- to late thirties and early forties. While perhaps shocking by current standards, that figure is consistent with life expectancy throughout most of Europe and colonial states in the New World. In all cases, when compared with more modern death rates, higher infant mortality kept the median death rate high. Further, the overall health of the presidio population may have been somewhat better than those Europeans living in urban areas with poor hygiene. Worldwide, urban dwellers were more susceptible to pathogens and epidemics.

Chapter 10

BURIAL PATTERNS AT THE CAMPO SANTO AND CHAPEL

How a culture or a related group of people treat their deceased reflects their spiritual beliefs, economic status and cultural values. One advantage of the data for burials at the presidio is that, with possible exceptions, after complete abandonment and burials in the 1870s, the population were Catholics given last rites and buried in a consecrated Catholic cemetery or in the chapel itself. In other words, the method of burial would have followed the common religious and cultural patterns of that singular population. Exceptions to that, which would include non-Catholics, would not be part of this study because no burials were archaeologically recovered beyond the chapel or outside of the recognized cemetery. Twenty-six individuals were buried in the chapel, including seventeen in the nave itself, four in the baptistry, three in the side chapel and one each in the sacristy and courtyard.

One interesting discovery was that of an amputated leg on the extreme southern edge of the cemetery, distant from other burials. The leg burial comprised portions of the left femur, the left tibia and fibula and foot bones. The individual would have kept approximately two-thirds of his left leg. The bones exhibited an extreme osteoporotic condition, showing bone disease over a long period, probably leading to the amputation. A forensic specialist suggested that this person would have had a noticeable limp for years prior to the amputation. Cursory examination of the footless amputated bone showed that the leg had been cut with a moderately fine-toothed saw rather than a coarse-toothed saw. This may show that someone at the presidio had access to a medical kit. Regarding the owner of the amputated leg, no record of an amputee was found in the reviewed records.

Of the 126 burials that were archaeologically excavated or partially excavated (of the over 220 burials that appear in the mission death records), 100 were buried in the cemetery or in open ground (possibly unconsecrated ground) near the cemetery. The numerical discrepancy between burials recorded in the mission records and burials discovered archaeologically can be explained by several factors.

The remains of babies and the very young may have disintegrated rapidly. This would have been especially true for burials in the cemetery itself. Burials in this open ground would have been subject to groundwater seeping through the soils. After the area was grassed and made into a park, irrigation was installed and fertilizer applied on a regular basis. The increase in moisture and the chemicals in the fertilizer sped up the deterioration of the skeletal materials. A second reason for the numerical disparity is that the archaeological excavations may not have extended far enough south to uncover remains in that area. A third reason is that it is possible that at one time the cemetery extended to other parts of the presidio. At one point, well after the chapel and cemetery excavations ceased in 1976, cadaver dogs were employed beyond the known portions of the excavated cemetery. They repeatedly "sat," indicating subsurface human remains.

Most of the burials were in a supine position (on their back with their face and torso upward) situated with their head positioned to the east. Typically, hands were folded across the chest or abdomen and ankles commonly crossed over each other. This configuration is consistent with data on the burials from Mission La Purisima near Santa Barbara, California, the only other Spanish colonial mission for which there is substantial published interment data.

By contrast, at Mission San Diego de Alcalá in Mission Valley, most of the burials uncovered in a 1989 excavation within a portion of that church's campo santo were pointed in a north/northeastern direction. They did, however, exhibit hands folded across their chests. At the presidio, placement of the head tilted to one side or the other occurred, but rarely.

Exceptions to the eastern orientation of the burials at the presidio may reflect post-abandonment interments. These would include Burial 2, probably a sailor, in the front portion of the nave and Burial 3 within the chapel directly in front of the side chapel. These two burials were interred at a right angle to most other burials. Burial 7, interred contiguous to and parallel to the altar, and Burial 23, buried east of the priest's quarters in the old courtyard and cooking area, were also buried more to the north than to the east. It is likely that these burials reflect death and burial after regular services were held at the presidio chapel, probably post-abandonment. Burial 23, discovered in what was once the courtyard, was a female Native American buried in the 1870s.

The average depth of the presidio burials was four to six feet below ground surface at the time of burial, although some, possibly later, burials were between three and four feet in depth. Most of the interments were with no enclosure (e.g. a coffin) or with merely a burial shroud or blanket. One soldier was buried in a horsehair blanket, possibly his saddle blanket. At least two females had lace and filigree shrouds. Approximately twenty-one of the burials were in wooden coffins, with eleven being hexagonal and six simple rectangular.

Use of hexagonal coffins apparently does not reflect a particular period given that Burial 7, assumed to be Joseph M. Arroyo, was in a hexagonal coffin, and he was buried in November 1775; the Fitch burials (Burial 12 and 16) from the 1840s were also in hexagonal coffins. Four coffins, given their disintegration, were of indeterminate shape. The twenty-one coffin burials is a higher number than the six coffin burials suggested earlier in a report by Greta and Paul Ezell, but at the time, the couple had knowledge of fewer than twenty-five burials. Suitable wood for coffins was difficult to procure in frontier San Diego. The 1777 and 1783 Inventario for Mission San Diego lists coffins "big" and "small" but does not note the type of wood or origin. Coffins, or wood for coffins, including redwood, may have been shipped down from Monterey along with other supplies.

Burial goods associated with the remains that were archaeologically excavated varied. This variance probably reflects gender and social status. Catholic doctrine discouraged ostentatious funerary goods. The most common burial item was a simple crucifix, often with rosary beads. Rings and bracelets were uncommon; they were probably removed prior to the burial. Glass beads were present and may have been ornamentation on a garment or strung on a necklace. Both Native burials and non-Native burials contained glass beads.

One of the female Native American burials, age thirty-five to forty years, had over thirty glass beads buried with her. One bead was a green tube-shaped bead, and the others were shades of powder and dark blue. Several metallic medallions may have also been associated with burials. At least one of the female Native American burials had an abalone pendant associated with it and may have been a later burial. For the Kumeyaay, abalones were spiritual creatures. It was said that if you talked to a living abalone, they would sometimes provide you with insights and messages.

One male, Burial 93, had a Cottonwood Triangular arrow point lodged in his right shoulder. He was laid to rest in the cemetery approximately ten feet beyond the southern wall of the chapel. While speculative, the burial may be that of Joseph Urselino, who was killed along with Jose Arroyo in the mission raid in November 1775. Urselino's death record states he died from at least one arrow wound to the groin. Whether he had other arrow wounds was not stated.

For the one hundred burials excavated within the cemetery rather than within the chapel (seventeen burials), sacristy (one burial), side chapel (three burials), baptistry (four burials) and courtyard (one burial), there was evidence of severe disturbance caused by the excavation of later burial pits and deposition of trash. It is probable that over the over five decades of use as a burial ground, grave markers—probably simple wooden crosses—became displaced or lost and the grave diggers, probably lower-ranking soldiers or Indian laborers, would have dug into previous graves before realizing their mistake.

Sometimes, it appears that the bones of previous burials were pushed aside to make room for another burial. Readers of Shakespeare's *Hamlet* may

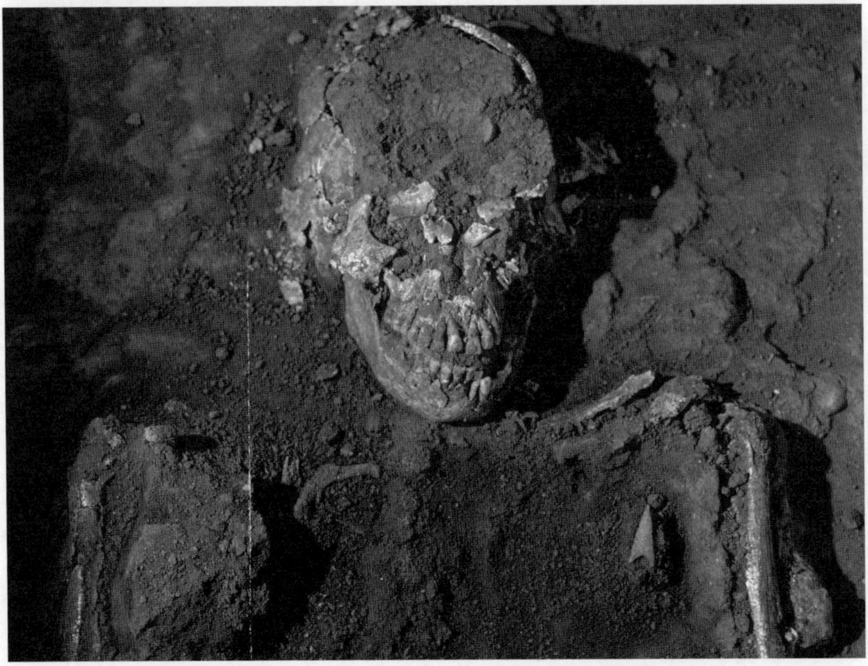

Probably carpenter José Urselino with arrow point in his upper left shoulder. *Author's collection.*

be familiar with the graveyard scene in Act V. The grave digger excavating a fresh grave for Ophelia encounters a mass of bones and a skull. One skull is identified as Yorick, Hamlet's jester. Hamlet tells his friend Horatio that he knew Yorick well. The men solemnly ponder life and death, and the skull is thrown back into the grave. Later, Ophelia will be laid to rest among the disturbed bones. At the presidio, untold numbers of burials may lay scattered unseen beneath archaeologically documented interments.

For those people buried within the chapel (nave, baptistry, sanctuary, side chapel and sacristy), interesting chronological indicators were noted. It is possible that some of the early burials (pre-1781) predated the construction of Lieutenant Zúñiga's adobe church, which was completed in 1783. In those instances, the burials may have been literally tiled over to accommodate the larger church beyond the footprint of the earlier churches. Evidence for this lies in the burial record that note burials "en la Iglesia" (in the church) prior to construction of Zúñiga's chapel. Some of the subfloor burials had a layer of sand between them and the floor tiles. That layer of sand may have been placed on the uneven surface before the tiles were mortared in place.

In other instances, several of the burials were placed in the ground after the floor tiles had been initially laid and mortared. The floor tiles were apparently chiseled or dug out, the grave excavated and the deceased lowered into the ground (with or without a coffin), and then soil was shoveled back in and the tiles were replaced and re-mortared. In general, this pattern probably shows a post-1783 date, when the chapel construction was completed, and pre-1835 burial, reflecting that the religious structures were still in use and that, for cultural and aesthetic purposes, the floor was repaired. By contrast, some burials beneath the tile floors exhibited replacement of the tiles on top of the burial pit but without careful placement and re-mortaring of the tiles. This probably reflects post-abandonment burial in the 1830s. The last church recorded burial in the chapel was that of José María Estudillo, a married man, in April 1830.

Based on archaeological evidence, at least twenty-five people were buried within the church itself, typically in the nave area. The archaeological data showing twenty-five people is close to the thirty-four burials recorded in mission records. Three people were interred in the sanctuary, including one individual (Burial 7) buried beneath the altar platform itself. At least four burials, including Burial 97, were buried in the southern baptistry, and at least three burials (Burials 5, 6 and 15) were in the northern side chapel.

The side chapel may have been commissioned by Felipe Romero, the presidio blacksmith, and it is where two of his children are buried. Side chapels were often paid for or built by families with the means to do so. Throughout Mexico and Spain, these side chapels are essentially family chapels. This may have been the case for Felipe and Rosalia Marquez, his wife. Their son Joseph Romero was buried in the little room in 1785. That would be consistent with archaeological evidence that the side chapel was cut into the relatively new 1783 Zúñiga chapel. Joseph's sister Maria Josepha was interred there in 1797, virtually on top of her brother. In excavating her grave after removing the floor tiles, the digger badly disturbed her brother's remains to a point of severe disarticulation. Shades of poor Yorick.

A single burial (Burial 8) was noted in the sacristy. Regarding burials within a California church or chapel, California historian Hubert H. Bancroft suggested that the practice of burying persons in the chapel was discouraged by the priests in 1797. A single burial was recorded within the mission records as in the chapel as late as 1830. The decedent was José María Estudillo, a cavalry captain. The recovery of twenty-five burials through archaeological excavation in the chapel and mission death and burial records, noting thirty-four such burials, offers an interesting gap between the written record and the archaeological record.

In contrast to what researchers suggested early in the excavations, neither social status nor gender was associated with burial in the chapel. It is possible that as at Santa Barbara Presidio, the chapel was typically used for the earliest burials, with later burials taking placing in consecrated ground to the south of the chapel. Certainly, the burial of what is assumed to be Joseph Arroyo in 1775 but apparently re-interred within the sanctuary at the foot of the altar around the time of completion of the 1783 chapel reflects early usage of the religious structure. This continued until about 1827, although such use tapered off after 1797. Burials in the chapel after the 1830s, such as the Fitches and Snook (see following discussion), do not appear in the mission records.

Of the burials known from mission death and burial records to be buried in the chapel, fourteen were adult males, including twelve Hispanics and two Natives from Baja California. One of the Native men included Fabian, the highly regarded Cochimi from San Fernando de Velicatá previously discussed. Five adult females were buried in the chapel, including three Hispanics and two Natives.

Eleven children were buried in the chapel, although more specifically, María Josepha Romero and Joseph María Romero, the young children of the presidio blacksmith and armorer Felipe Romero, were buried in the

side chapel that extended from the north wall of the chapel proper. Interestingly, only one of the decedent children buried in the chapel was identified as Indio—a child of five years old named Pedro Fages. He died in December 1776, and while listed as Indio, there has been some speculation that he was the mestizo son of Lieutenant Pedro Fages and a Kumeyaay woman. This speculation may have arisen from the fact that Lieutenant Fages served as the child's *padrino*, or godfather, at his baptism. Naming a newborn after the padrino or padrina was common practice. A non-Españole child buried in the chapel was a mestizo boy, Nabor Antonio Cota. Cota was the son of a soldier and a Native woman (Gabrielino-Tongva) from San Juan Capistrano/San Gabriel.

José Francisco Snook, known previously as Joseph Frank Snook before his conversion to Catholicism and Mexican citizenship, was buried in 1848 in a wooden coffin within the western end (entranceway) of the chapel. His initials "JFS" were carefully spelled out in brass tacks purchased from his friend Henry Fitch's store in the pueblo. Henry Delano Fitch, an important American merchant and sea captain, and his youngest daughter, Natalia, were also buried in the front (western) entry to the presidio chapel nave in 1849 and 1845, respectively, after abandonment of the presidio.

By the time of Henry Fitch's burial, the chapel's adobe walls had begun to melt, as evidenced by his grave being excavated through the adobe "melt" on the floor of the nave. Unlike the Spanish- and Mexican-era burials, the Fitches were buried in redwood coffins with formal hinges. Their initials (HDF and NF) were carefully tapped on the coffin lids by brass tacks, probably from his own store. Hearts formed out of tacks were also tapped into their coffin lids. In contemporary thought, hearts represented love and truth but also symbolized where a person finds God. The tacks on Natalia's lid were in near perfect condition. Henry Fitch's coffin was clad in tooled leather, an unusual burial feature.

Opposite: Coffin lid of Natalia Fitch with copper tacks spelling out her initials and forming hearts. *Author's collection.*

Above: Grave and coffin lid of José Francisco Snook with brass tack initials, "JFS." *Author's collection.*

It is probable that non-Christianized Indians who died in the presidio prison, including the Kumeyaay rebel patriot Naguasajo and other non-Catholic rebels and at least one Protestant fur trapper, Sylvester Pattie, were buried beyond the Catholics' consecrated grounds. These areas were not subject to archaeological investigation, and of course, the deaths of non-Catholics do not appear in the mission death records. A plaque to Sylvester Pattie is mounted on the replica of the southeastern bastion within the corner of the presidio. The exact final resting place of these men remains one of the many mysteries of Presidio Park.

Archaeological investigations revealed that two Native American adult male burials (Burial 87 and Burial 121) were dispatched by lead musket balls. Burial 87 has a musket ball on the right side of the thorax region just above the collarbone. Burial 121 has two musket balls lodged just below the neck region in the extreme upper chest and a crucifix near the chest. Burial 87 was situated beneath the subfloor on the south side of the nave near the entrance to the baptistry and was estimated to be between twenty-five and thirty-five years of age. Burial 121 was within the cemetery between the baptistry and the outer defense wall. No estimate of age was provided. These burials most likely represent two of the four Kumeyaay men who are known to have been executed between 1813 and 1826 and buried at the presidio.

Given that the person associated with Burial 87 died between twenty-five and thirty-five years of age, it may be associated with Native men roughly of that age who are known to have been executed. These men are Juan Bautista Guaycupuchal, age thirty; Tiburcio, age forty; or possibly Anciento, for whom no data is available for his age at the time of death. At forty-six years of age, Vicente Meyapapuchal is less likely to be Burial 87. Lacking solid forensic data for Burial 121, it is not possible to correlate that burial with an individual, although as with Burial 87, it is likely one of the four executed Kumeyaay men.

Chapter 11

INDIGENOUS PEOPLE IN THE ARCHAEOLOGICAL RECORD

Introduction

Given the sometimes-scant written information about Indigenous people at the San Diego Presidio, is it possible to learn more about these people? After all, they played important roles as wives, workers, artists and, yes, even prisoners. As described in a previous chapter, Indigenous people are clearly documented in the archival and historical records for the presidio. These written records, however, generally note only the important time markers of their life, such as birth and baptism, marriage and death. A list of converted Kumeyaay at the mission, which probably applies to the presidio, lists the following occupations: vaquero, carpenter, blacksmith, fisherman, shoemaker, butcher and chocolate maker. In other words, the converted neophytes were far more than just laborers.

The Indigenous presence, as reflected in the archaeological record, adds another important level of understanding. Their lives and contributions run through the very fiber of Spanish and Californio history and culture at the site. Consider the Native or mixed-blood women who bore children from Hispanic or mestizo fathers. Those women produced the next generation of soldiers, artisans, vaqueros and workers. A significant portion of the early San Diego pueblo had ties not only to the presidio and to Mexico but also to traditional Native villages and landscapes.

Lacking the written word, archaeology cannot just fill in some blanks, it can provide an interwoven picture of daily life, art forms, burial patterns and the interaction with non-Native peoples. There is much that can be teased out from discarded food waste, ornaments, forensic evaluation of skeletal material and virtually every item touched, made, used and lost at the presidio.

An important and overlooked non-burial cultural item includes altered floor and roof tiles manufactured by Native artisans. As a result of more than a decade of excavations at the San Diego Presidio chapel complex (mission chapel, priests' quarters, cemetery and courtyard), almost twenty examples of incised or inscribed tiles were recovered and catalogued. The specimens varied from nearly complete floor and roof tiles to fragments of floor tiles. Most incised tiles at the presidio came from within the chapel itself, some in direct association with architectural features.

In several instances, Native artisans inscribed wet clay with designs and symbols. In most of the examples at the presidio, the inscriptions were apparently made with a finger, although a few examples were drawn with a stick or a stylus. Known as inscriptive art, examples of this artistic expression were more than examples of Native doodles as earlier portrayed. Some researchers and art historians have suggested that at least some of the paintings and artwork performed by California Indians in the missions were what they termed "abusive" art—that is, unauthorized artwork completed by and for the Indians rather than as part of the regimented mission decorations.

A borderlands historian suggested that not just in the California missions but all over the world, colonized people used art to mock and sometimes condemn their oppressors. This author would agree and suggests that at the San Diego Presidio and Mission San Diego, inscriptive art is a successful Tipai attempt to inject their own meanings and symbols into the intrusive Catholic Church and Spanish military.

One of the potentially more evocative incised tiles is only a fragment. It is possible that this tile, which is finger-incised, depicts a human figure, possibly a robed priest or a helmeted soldier. Apart from this tile, there are no other known tile designs from the presidio that appear to illustrate a human or anthropomorphic figure. Even in pre-contact eras, Kumeyaay rock painting and etchings rarely depicted human figures.

Several of the roof tiles have designs on them that are stylistically different from the floor tile designs. One tile shows vertical and horizontal linear designs that formed a fiber or woven motif. Apparently, the lines were inscribed using some form of a flattish stylus. A second roof tile has a series of four parallel lines running left to right diagonally across the tile. A set

Left: Wavy lines incised into clay floor tile at the time of manufacture. *Author's collection.*

Right: Incised lines in clay tile. Possibly a priest or a soldier. *Author's collection.*

of similar, although fainter and shallower, lines appear to cross the more dominant lines, resulting in a semi-cross hatch effect. Given the curved, concave nature of the incising, a finger probably served as the stylus for this example. It is interesting to speculate why anyone would decorate a tile that could only be seen from above the chapel.

A third curved tile, which may have been a cylindric clay water pipe, exhibits what rock art scholars might call "scratched" lines. The lines are much thinner than those found on other tiles at the presidio and appear to form curvilinear shapes. The clay water pipes may have been buried beneath the courtyard to carry floodwater away from the church.

Apparently unique to the presidio, an incised floor tile depicting what appears to be a ship and a tile with a sketch of the presidio itself were also discovered. As of this writing, the tile depicting the ship cannot be located. A broken tile depicting the contours of Presidio Hill measures ten inches by eleven inches. The image extends across the length of the tile. The inscription was done with a pointed object, rather than a finger, that left one-eighth-inch-wide lines. A series of two wavy lines that crisscross each other form what appear to be the hills and valleys to the south of Mission Valley.

Protruding from the hill in the background to the right is a straight vertical line with what is clearly a rectangular inscription with internal lines that converge toward the center of what may be a flag. Although the design contained within the rectangle does not resemble the Spanish flag from circa

Incised tile with possible depiction of Presidio Hill and Spanish army flag. *Author's collection.*

1769 to 1821 or the subsequent Mexican national flag after 1821, it shares some attributes with the Spanish army flag from the Spanish era. Was this tile art the work of a Native artisan or a Spanish worker?

The presence of inscriptive art throughout several California missions clearly shows an ongoing trans–Native American art form. Probably underreported, incised and impressed tiles occur at Mission La Purísima, Mission Santa Barbara and Mission San Antonio de Padua farther to the north. This expression of traditional and acculturative art provides insights into Indigenous culture during the colonial period. The inscriptions may be seen, as they apparently were by the mission fathers and presidial soldiers, as doodles or as meaningless designs executed by bored Native workers. Far more likely, the designs reflect a cultural continuity of Native art expressed in a new medium.

Indigenous Vessels

Another Native art form found at the presidio, although of a more utilitarian nature, is thousands of Tizon brown ware (San Diego brown) ceramic sherds. The superb multi-volume monumental study conducted on colonial and Native wares at the presidio chapel by Steve Van Wormer, Susan Wade and Susan Walter showed that although a wide variety of European and Asian ceramics were owned and used by the presidio inhabitants, Native wares were more common. Vessels, such as cooking pots, bowls and water storage containers, were brought into the presidio and used, probably by Native and non-Native alike. With the exceptions noted below, the vessel types stayed traditional, reflecting the forms and styles the Kumeyaay women had been making for generations.

One remarkable discovery of the Van Wormer, Wade and Walter study was *cazuelas* and *comales* manufactured from local clays, thus providing a Tizon brown ware cooking platform. Traditionally, cazuelas in Spain and comales in Mexico are made from terra cotta and used as relatively shallow

Top: Tizon brown ware vessel of the type used at the presidio. *Stephen Van Wormer*.

Bottom: Tizon brown ware olla of the type made and used at the presidio. *Stephen Van Wormer.*

pots for cooking or serving stews and soups. The Tizon cazuelas from the presidio were manufactured using traditional paddle and anvil techniques reflecting Native adaptability.

The origin of the Native vessels at the presidio is uncertain. Some may have been brought into the presidio by Native workers or by Kumeyaay wives with contacts at nearby villages. Given the sheer number of Native vessels, some number of them must have been made specifically to service the needs of the men and women of the presidio. It is an intriguing possibility that some of the ceramic vessels reflect items that were traded or bartered for goods available at the presidio, such as glass beads, cloth and metal. Clearly, trade was taking place between Native people beyond the presidio walls and its inhabitants. In 1811, Father Panto, stationed at the mission, requested of the presidio commander, Francisco Ruiz, that all trade between Native people and the presidio be approved by the priests. It is unlikely that Ruiz enforced that edict, believing that Panto was overstepping his authority.

Abalone shellfish hooks. *Dennis Gallegos.*

Specific examples of Kumeyaay manufacturing nontraditional vessel types include molded ceramic slabs for grilling and cooking called comales. Comales are still used in Mexico to warm or cook tortillas. At least one shaped steatite (soapstone) comale was uncovered at the presidio. The steatite was most likely sourced from a large quarry in the Cuyamaca Mountains, over fifty miles to the east. Less likely, although possible, is that the source was the Channel Islands near Santa Barbara. Native ceramics were also formed into a nontraditional taza or flat-bottomed bowl and at least one *pocillo* or cup. These examples of syncretic Native behavior clearly reflect the adaptability of the Kumeyaay. In these instances, it is not so much that the Natives were becoming acculturated as that they were responding to demand for such products.

Other items that can be associated with Native occupants include abalone pendants, abalone fishhooks, arrow points, manos and metates made from local stone and other stone tools. It is also likely that Kumeyaay hunters and fishers supplied some portion of the wild game such as deer, shellfish and fish cooked and eaten at the presidio. Fisherman was one of the occupations listed for neophytes at the mission and later in the San Diego pueblo.

In at least one instance, the presidio commandant, Fernando Rivera y Moncada, traded glass beads that he had brought from Mexico to Iipai villagers several miles to the north of the presidio for fish. This event took place in July 1776 in a period of extremely low food supplies at the presidio. Moncada reported in his diary that he sent Sergeant Ortega to the coastal village of Onap (San Buenaventura) to barter for fish. The trade went well, and Ortega returned with saddlebags full of fish.

A combination of archaeological discoveries and archival research illuminates the Native presence at the presidio. These people were not necessarily slaves. They were wives, artisans, paid laborers, valets, bricklayers and fishermen. Native women did domestic chores as expected in the period, bore children and, sometimes, entered widowhood. Native men, in addition to the roles noted above, were sometimes imprisoned, executed and even exiled. The presidio was a microcosm of the colonial landscape.

Chapter 12

COLONIAL ARTIFACTS AND ARCHITECTURE

Introduction

Years before the term *globalization* became a common word in economic vocabulary, an early form of globalization took place at the San Diego Presidio. With its sheltered harbor and favorable location between the Northern California settlements and the supply depots in Baja California and mainland Mexico, the occupants of San Diego had access to goods from much of the world. Access to outside goods shifted over six decades of occupation at the presidio, especially after the Mexican revolution in 1821. Archival documents and archaeological discoveries paint a picture of relative abundance and variety in material goods.

Ceramics

Perhaps nothing better reflects the variety of artifact types made, imported, used and discarded than ceramics. As one might expect, given over seventy years of occupation, the occupants of the presidio used ceramic objects and vessels from all over the world. San Diego was on the frontier, but with its excellent harbor, its occupants had access to ships from several foreign ports. Certainly, those from mainland Mexico were the most common, but ceramic vessels from China, England, France, America and elsewhere adorned their tables and shelves. In contrast to early Spanish settlements in the Floridian-

Caribbean region, ceramics did not have to be imported from Spain. By the early 1700s, Mexico possessed a thriving ceramic industry centered on Tlaquepaque and Puebla.

While few intact or even nearly intact historic ceramic vessels were recovered at the presidio, thousands of sherds reflecting a wide assortment of ceramic types were found. The context of the ceramics varied from somewhat discrete trash deposits (the chapel courtyard and the gateway) to dispersion within the variously disturbed levels of the overall site. Trash deposits at the Chapel and Gateway Excavation have been studied in detail.

The following discussion applies to both deposits, but the fine details are based on the Chapel Excavation. This discussion pulls heavily from the exemplary work titled *Shadows of the Things That Have Been: An Analysis of and Identification Guide to Ceramics from the Chapel Complex Excavation of the San Diego Presidio*, authored by Stephen R. Van Wormer, Sue A. Wade and Susan D. Walter. Most of the narrative regarding non-Native ceramics presented below is directly taken from their work. Their multivolume work is available online through Academia.

Predominantly comprising Maiolica ware manufactured in Mexico, with lesser amounts of Canton and English wares, the vessel types used at the presidio reflect utilitarian uses and mid-level economic status. The Maiolicas—which can also be spelled Majolica or Mayolica—included examples of what early researchers called the five Puebla phases. Five types were noted: Puebla I 1700–50 (Puebla blue-on-white and wavy rim blue-on-white), Puebla II and III 1750–1800 (San Elizario polychrome and San Diego polychrome), Puebla IV 1800–20 (Tucumcari polychrome) and Puebla V 1830–1900 (Mexican polychrome). Inventories for Mission San Diego, and by association for the presidio, record a variety of Puebla wares, including bowls, cups, plates and saucers.

Galera ware is a traditional utilitarian Mexican lead-glazed redware used for table settings, vases, cooking and a variety of other culinary and domestic functions. This porous low-fired earthenware was sealed with lead glazing to make the vessel impervious to liquids. This overglaze helped preserve painted decorations from chipping or use wear. Galera is still in popular use throughout Mexico as cooking vessels and tableware. There are several varieties of Galera, including undecorated, which, at the chapel, was the dominant type.

In many ways, monochrome clear glazed Galera ware is like the Maiolica serving and tableware described above. Vessels of this type are covered with a clear glaze on the interior and sometimes on the exterior. The brownish-

Mexican Galera ware.
Stephen Van Wormer.

orange to beige body paste takes on a bright orange appearance where it has been glazed. Under glaze designs in the form of dotted petals, solid, wavy and solid single- and multiple-band rim treatments were hand painted rather than stenciled. Dots, spirals and nested or stacked crescents were applied in shades of dark brown to black.

Tonalá Bruñida is an unglazed, slip-decorated, highly burnished earthenware. It appears in relatively small frequencies on many Mexican colonial and early republic period sites in California, the southwestern United States, Texas, Florida, Mexico and the Caribbean. As with many Mexican ceramic wares, it is known by a variety of terms, including Guadalajara polychrome, Tonalá ware, Tonalá polychrome, Tonalá Bruñida ware, Bruñida de Tonalá ware and Tonalá burnished ware. In Mexico, it is often called Bruñida, Barro Bruñida and occasionally Loza de Olor. In the eighteenth and nineteenth centuries it was called Loza de Guadalajara, Loza de Olor, Bucaro de Guadalajara and Bucaro.

The porous fine cream, tan or gray-colored paste in Tonalá shows no obvious tempering. Vessel exteriors are covered with a fine white, tan or pink clay slip, which serves as a background for colored slip applied decorations in a variety of colors, including blue-gray, black and various shades of red and orange. Designs consist of thin delicate rectilinear, floral and curvilinear elements, geometric forms and animal motifs, with exterior bands on most of the rims and around the bases. The surfaces of some sherds are entirely red or black on one surface. This exterior was burnished or polished with a stone, giving the vessels a subdued sheen. Some interior treatments exhibit simple smoothed surfaces, while others were slipped and burnished.

Fifty-eight sherds of Tonalá Bruñida ware were recovered from the Chapel Excavation. Twenty-two distinct vessels and other objects were identified through analysis of pattern designs, body shape, rim diameter and paste color. Tonalá Bruñida ware items included hollowwares, plates, figurines and a candleholder. Hollowwares dominated and comprised five escudilla-style bowls (almost 23 percent) a saucer (4.5 percent) and two small, mouthed vessels (10 percent). Three flatware platos (almost 14 percent) and five unidentified vessels (almost 23 percent) made up the rest of the table and serving ware assemblages. There was also a candle holder (4.5 percent) and limbs of two figurines (9 percent).

Maiolica is an earthenware with a vitreous, opaque enamel surface made with tin and lead oxide. Like Galera wares, since lead leaches through clay surfaces at even low temperatures, hot meals prepared and served in these containers produced high levels of toxicity. Mexican Maiolicas are part of a distinctively Hispanic category of glazed, wheel-thrown ceramics known by a variety of terms, including majolica, Mayolica, maiolica, Talavera and tin-enameled or tin-glazed earthenware. In México proper, they are called Talavera, Talavera Poblana, Talavera de Puebla, mayólica, loza estannífera and loza blanca. In eighteenth-century shipping orders and inventories, they were often listed as simply loza or Puebla.

Maiolicas are characterized by a soft earthenware paste covered by opaque vitreous enamel or glaze. The addition of tin oxide to the lead glaze produces an opacity that is also found on French Faience and English and Dutch delftware. The glaze is usually white, although yellow, blue and other colors can occur. On decorated pieces, metal oxides painted onto the glazed surface between the first and second firing create a variety of distinct, colorful designs. The following are the major subsets of Maiolica.

Puebla blue-on-white and blue polychrome are subsets of Maiolica. The Puebla blue-on-white and blue-on-white polychrome traditions are characterized by blue design motifs on a white background. Polychrome traditions express themselves with black/brown accent lines. San Agustín blue-on-white identified in California and Arizona is not the same ceramic design as that recognized as San Agustín blue-on-white in other regions. That is the justification for using the hyphenated designation San Agustín–molded blue-on-white used in local regional studies.

San Elizario polychrome is like Puebla blue-on-white except that "brownish black" emphasis lines have been added beside or on top of the blue. *Platos* (plates) have broad blue rim bands with the brown/black accent lines. A row of blue petals runs along the bottom of the band. Stylized floral motifs

Left: Monochrome ware. *Right*: San Elizario ware. *Susan Walter and Stephen Van Wormer.*

are interspersed along the row of petals. The central medallion frequently exhibits a blue crane-like bird. Brown/black accents are used for the legs and beak on the bird motif and/or on blue petals and flowers.

Monterey polychrome–type ceramic is recognized by its stylized cornstalk motifs used along the sides and as the central medallion. On the platos, three are evenly spaced along the inside of the vessel below the orange rim band. Each is flanked by baroque-like flourishes and elongated, light green floral sprays. A set of cornstalks and floral sprays is separated by a green diamond. Another orange band surrounds the stylized cornstalk central base medallion, which is enclosed with a ring of green dots.

San Diego polychrome orange exhibits a rim band with black accent lines. Unlike many other Aranama tradition wares, this type has free-floating elements comprising leaf-like or flower petal–like decorations executed in orange, yellow, green and blue. The elements are often outlined in black accents and connected by free-flowing scrolls in black and green. Cobalt blue dots are sometimes used as accent dots or filters. Central medallion elements include geometric patterns, elaborate stylized plants and anthropomorphic figures. Human figures are drawn in a style like Santa Cruz polychrome.

Huejotzingo straight-rim band is a Maiolica type characterized by a single blue, green or orange band encircling and slightly over the rim. It is on the inside rim of plates and the outside rim of taza cups. There are no other decorations. Only blue and green band decorated vessels were identified for the Chapel Complex collection. Fifty-one sherds (slightly more than 3

Left: Monterey ware. *Right*: San Diego ware. *Susan Walter and Stephen Van Wormer.*

percent) represented seven (almost 5 percent) plates. Five with blue edge decoration had eleven-inch rim diameters. Two green edge–decorated specimens exhibited a nine-and-one-half-inch rim diameter.

Huejotzingo wavy-rim band Maiolica is characterized by a single blue, green or orange band around the rim. The lower edge of the band is wavy or undulating. It is on the inside rim of platos and the outside rim of taza cups. Only blue and green wavy band decorated vessels were identified for the Chapel Complex collection.

Fourteen vessels were identified from eighty-three sherds. Blue wavy-rim decorated items included an escudilla bowl with a five- to six-inch rim diameter, a four-inch diameter taza cup and ten plates with nine-and-one half-inch rim diameters. Two green wavy-rim decorated platos also had a rim diameter of nine and one-half inches.

In total, the Maiolica assemblage recovered at the presidio produced a minimum number of 148 individual vessels. Puebla blue-on-white tradition decorated vessels were dominant, with 64 items composing 43 percent of the collection. A category labeled as "other traditions" made up 42 dishes, or 28 percent. There were 27 Aranama polychrome dishes, at 18 percent. Last, Poblano/fine line traditions make up 15 items, composing 10 percent of the collection.

The Maiolica assemblage from the Chapel Complex consists almost exclusively of tableware. Of the vessel forms, eighty-three plates dominate the functional types, composing 56 percent of the vessel assemblage. Forty-three escudilla (shallow soup plate)-style bowls made up 29 percent, while nineteen cups (tazas, jícaras, pocillos) represented almost 13 percent. The only non-tableware items are a single escudilla/jar and two unidentified vessels that make up less than 2 percent of the Maiolica collection. Tazas and escudillas (cups and bowls) combined represented sixty-two vessels, or almost 42 percent of the assemblage.

Vessel form and specific pattern types bore some associations. Puebla blue-on-white shows a strong relationship to escudilla bowls and taza and jícara cups. Among the forty-three escudillas, nineteen Puebla blue-on-white decorated examples made up 45 percent, or almost one-half, of the assemblage. Among the nineteen tazas and jícaras, Puebla blue-on-white decorated vessels were the highest-ranking type at 26 percent. Additional significant associations for escudillas include eight Puebla white and seven combined Aranama patterned vessels that represented 19 and 17 percent, respectively, while for cups (tazas, jícaras and pocillos), a strong relationship with late Poblano Mexican fine line patterns exists at 21 percent of the assemblage.

Of the eighty-three platos, twenty-three San Elizario polychrome decorated vessels dominate at 27 percent. These are followed by twenty Huejotzingo straight (seven) and wavy-rim band (thirteen) items at 24 percent. As with the escudilla bowls, if all Aranama items are combined, they make up a major decorative category for the plates and represent twenty items, or 24 percent of the collection.

In summary, Puebla blue-on-white and Puebla white are mainly linked with escudilla bowls and taza and jícara cups. San Elizario polychrome and Huejotzingo edge decorated patterns are largely associated with platos. Aranama polychrome patterns show strong associations with platos and, to a lesser extent, escudillas. For whatever reason, there are no Aranama decorated cups (tazas, jícaras or pocillos).

The historical record offers glimpses into the ordering, shipment and use of ceramic wares at both the mission and the presidio. As early as 1777, Father Fermin Lausen reported "china" cups and one dozen "Puebla" plates at San Diego. Plates, cups and saucers of Puebla ware are repeatedly noted in the mission inventories. This importation of more than a small quantity of Maiolica at the San Diego Presidio and Mission San Diego may be significant when compared with other missions and presidios.

Some early scholars suggested presidios might produce more Mexican and European ceramic wares than would missions. In part, this would be because of the sheer number of troops (including more affluent officers) when compared to the few non-Native occupants at the missions. In theory at least, the mission priests sought simple tableware and serving dishes except for a few more elaborate pieces.

Botijas, often called olive jars, were coarse earthenware amphora-shaped vessels with narrow necks and mouth openings. They were sometimes coated on the inside with a lead glaze varying from emerald to olive green. On some vessels, the exteriors had a thin white slip. The paste color is usually reddish to pale tan. For slightly over three hundred years (1490–1800), they served as the main ceramic shipping container for the Spanish colonies. In Alta California, wine was carried from mission to mission or to the presidios in what was called *botijuelas*, a smaller-volume vessel than a botijas.

These botijas or botijuelas undoubtedly arrived as product containers aboard the San Blas supply ships. They were then kept and reused, the most likely secondary function being as *cántaros* or *tinajas* for water transport and storage and, as noted above, to hold wine. Acknowledgement of the varied uses of these vessels is important because too often their discovery on mission and presidio sites is associated solely with olive oil.

British ceramics at the presidio were apparently uneven, distributed with the largest quantity associated with the Chapel Complex, which may have included refuse from the commandant's quarters and the priest's rooms. Of all non-Native ceramics at the complex, 20 percent was British transferware. Compared to other missions and the San Francisco Presidio, these quantities are much higher.

Transferware is a term given to pottery that has had a pattern applied by transferring a print from a copper plate, then to paper and subsequently to the pottery body. This contrasts with more labor-intensive painted images or applied decals. This technique could produce a variety of colorful images relatively inexpensively.

British transferware came to the West Coast over several decades but probably reached its height at the presidio after trade restrictions were loosened post-1821. Trade into the Americas spawned a series of often poorly made ceramics with styles unique to the export market. Many of the styles and images on British transferware cannot be found in England.

The trade for British ceramics was just one element of an extensive hide and tallow trade based in California. Hides and tallow were traded to a spectrum of European countries, including England and Russia, as well as to the United States and Mexico. Ships from Europe and the United Kingdom would make stops in the Caribbean Islands, Mexico, Honolulu and Panama, where warehouses stocked goods from all over the world.

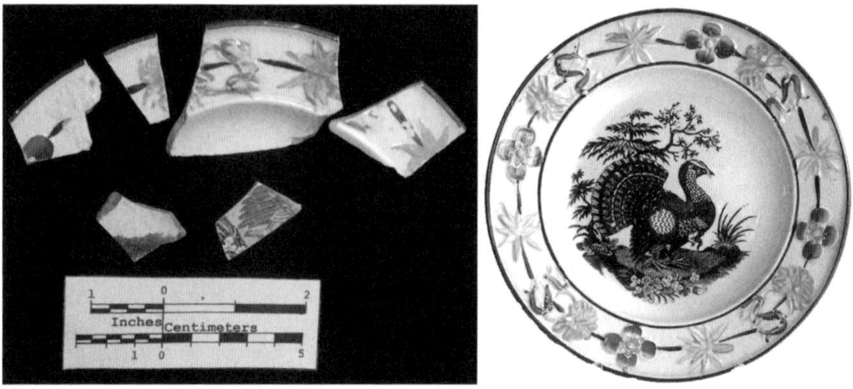

British turkey plate. *Stephen Van Wormer.*

British transferware at the presidio included goods manufactured by Spode, Wedgewood, Enoch Wood and Sons and several manufacturers based in Staffordshire. Vessel types included chamber pots, cups, saucers, plates, teapots and hollow ware. A wide variety of well-known designs is represented in the chapel collection. While not all-inclusive, examples of Tiber, Village Church, Trinity College Border, Trefoil Rim, Weeping Willow, White Stag and Waterfall were recovered. Generalized scenes include rural, pastoral and country estates, famous English buildings (London) and castles.

Within the recovered ceramics were examples of what may be categorized as children's ware. These are British manufactured plates and vessels that were produced and marketed for use by children. They typically feature whimsical images or sayings, including nursery rhyme snippets or children's homilies. One example is what is called a "turkey plate." This plate features a turkey in the center and a colorful border. A second example is a Staffordshire pearlware children's plate with a red transfer that reads "A Trifle for Thomas." Both plates and cups were made in this style, often called canary ware and sporting yellow pigments. This plate dates from approximately 1825, which fits well with the assumed increase in British trade goods coming to Alta California.

Other ceramics at the presidio included Chinese underglaze blue porcelains, Chinese overglaze enamel porcelains and English dark-colored creamware. Some suggest that in the late mission/early Mexican period, there was a shift in the use of ceramics and importation and use of English and Chinese wares gradually became dominant over the use of Maiolica.

Left: British Waterfall transferware from chapel excavation. *San Diego State University Collections Management Presidio Field Notes.*

Right: Children's British Thomas plate. *Stephen Van Wormer.*

This shift resulted from the weakening of Spanish-era trade restrictions and the overall increased trade with British and French merchants.

Local Native American brown ware pottery is an unglazed, usually undecorated, low-fired ceramic produced by Southern California Native artisans. Two major types were recovered at the San Diego Presidio: Tizon brown ware and, to a much lesser extent, lower Colorado buff ware. Both are pottery traditions with precontact origins.

Vessels were formed by coiling and shaped with a paddle and anvil. Often, an existing pot or basket was used to form the platform for the Tizon vessel base. Some of the ceramic sherds recovered at the presidio had basket fiber imprints in the vessel's base. Incising and painting were occasionally done, but rarely at the presidio. This may reflect the utilitarian nature of wares in the presidial households.

Brown ware was made from high iron–content residual granitic-derived clays of the Peninsular Range and takes on various shades of gray, brown to orange red after being fired under oxidizing conditions. A well-known clay source was in Spring Valley at the village of Metí, several miles east of the presidio. Several villagers from Metí had been baptized and had contact with both the mission and the presidio.

Firing was accomplished in an earth oven traditionally using oak bark as fuel. Introducing cattle led to some use of dried cow dung as fuel. Depending

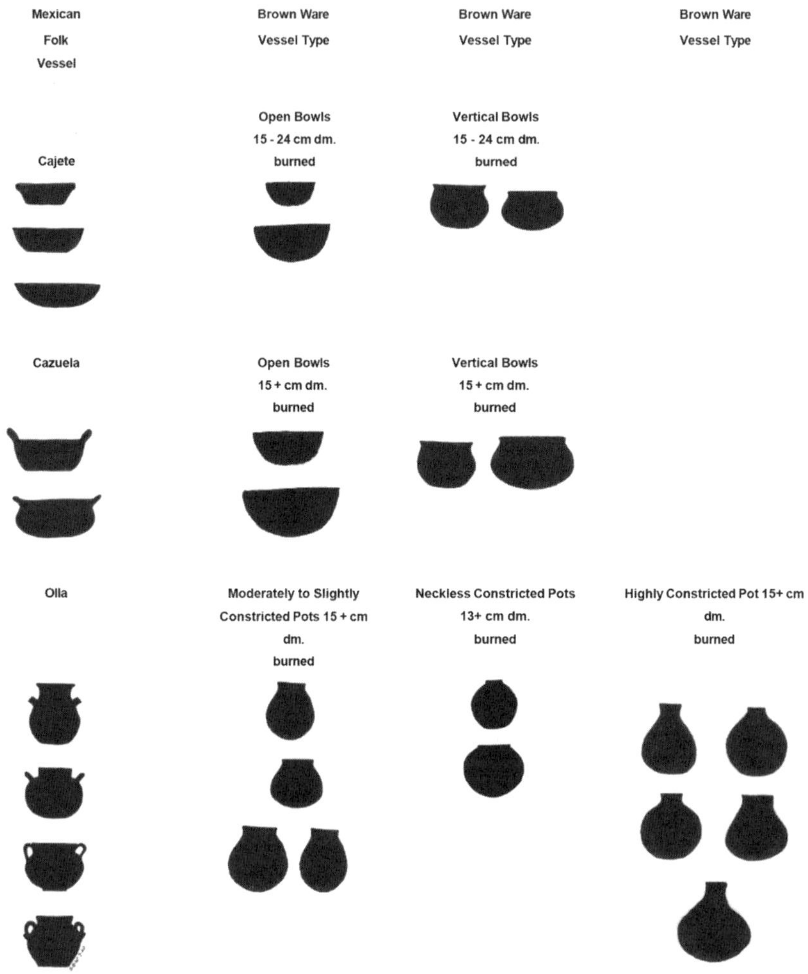

on the artisan (traditionally a woman) and the clay source, brown ware can have high to meager amounts of temper (sand, clay bits, quartz). The finer, thinner vessels have virtually no temper. Excavations at several Kumeyaay village sites occupied through the historic period have produced thousands of sherds of brown ware.

Formed from low iron–content sedimentary clays of Southern California's Colorado Desert, lower Colorado buff wares fire to colors of pink, buff, beige and gray. Buff wares have higher clay content and thinner walls. Buff wares are typically associated with the lower Colorado River tribes and the Quechan. The presence of buff ware in coastal San Diego, including at the

Opposite: Tizon brown ware vessel types and styles. *Stephen Van Wormer.*

Above: Man with a large olla and clay rattle. *Ramona Pioneer Historical Society.*

presidio, usually shows either trade with the river tribes or that a member of the river tribes was on site. It is interesting to note that at least two Native people at the presidio originated along the lower Colorado River.

As noted previously, a vast majority (99 percent) of the brown ware vessels identified showed no variations from traditional precontact forms. These included moderately to slightly constricted pots, neckless constricted pots, highly constricted pots, open bowls and vertical sided bowls. No examples of brown ware rattles or smoking pipes typically found at village sites were recovered.

Probable Mexican folk vessel functions represented included taza and pocillo cups, escudilla-style bowls, jarros, small and large cazuelas, cooking and serving cajete-style bowls, cooking ollas, serving ollas, cántaros and tinaja botellón water storage vessels. In most ways, the Tizon brown wares made for, and used at, the presidio were quite like traditional Mexican folk ware except for a few flat bottoms and few handles.

The presence of Tizon vessels and wares at the presidio with Spanish/ Mexican attributes and forms contrasts with the vessels discovered at the San Diego mission. Only a few Tizon wares reflected functional or stylistic changes. This may be because at the presidio, Kumeyaay women were the cooks preparing food for their husbands and family members in their own casitas. This could have led to more cultural continuity blended with attempts to adapt (to some degree) to the foods and cooking styles of their husbands.

Ollas, gaming discs, effigies and clay rattles were made by Kumeyaay artisans well into the late 1900s and probably much longer. In recent years, there has been a resurgence in Native ceramic manufacture on both sides of the Mexican border. Artisans south of the border never actually stopped making Native vessels and ware. Today, one can purchase Native Tipai ceramics at the Kosaii Indian Store in Old Town.

Glass and Glassware

Using glass for drinking vessels and for containers in general was not common in the early days of the presidio. Liquid items such as wine, brandy and olive oil were most frequently shipped to the region in wooden casks or relatively thick glazed brown ware (botijas), not in small-volume glass bottles. California, especially Mission San Diego and Mission San Gabriel, was producing fair-quality red wine and aguardiente, a type of brandy. Early inventories from between 1777 and 1790 do, however, list wine being shipped from Mexico, but not in glass.

At the presidio and the mission, some glass bottles associated with French wines and bottles known as junk bottles (brown or dark-colored thick glass vessels) were uncovered. Small tumblers were also present but only in relatively small numbers compared to ceramic vessels. No doubt wooden cups were also in use but have perished. Mission inventories also list metal cups and tankards, and these would have been in use at the presidio as well. Fine glassware or stemware, for which fragments have been recovered, was more likely to be used by the visiting priests, officials and ranking officers and not by the enlisted men. Mission inventories occasionally listed crystal glassware.

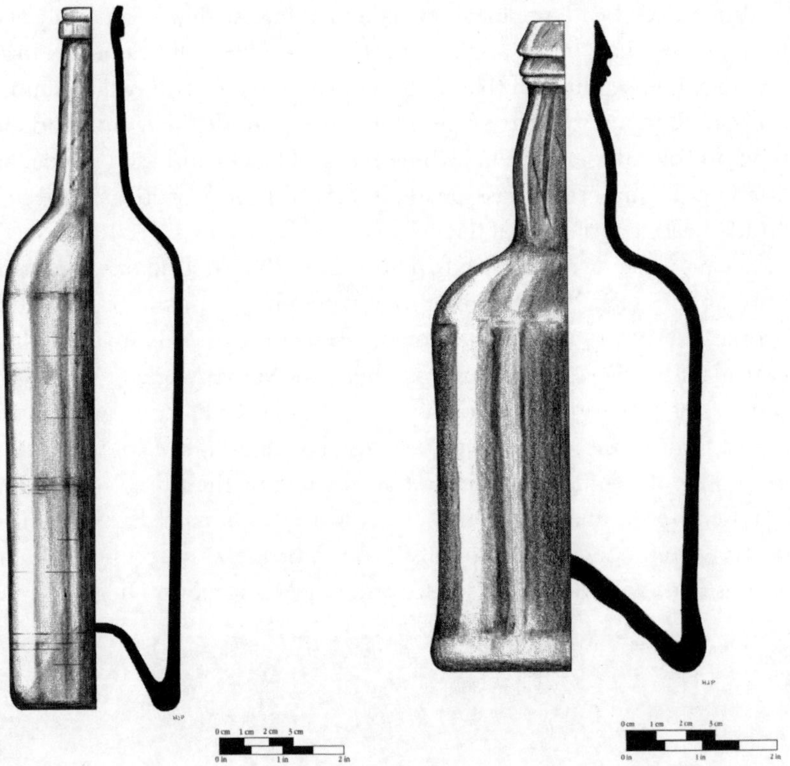

Left: Sketch of wine bottle. *Right*: Sketch of junk bottle. *Harry Price and Stephen Van Wormer.*

Personal Adornments: Beads

Glass beads at Spanish colonial sites represent far more than simple trade goods. In outlying settlements or rancherías, the beads may in fact have served as trade items between Spanish colonists and Natives and from Natives at the mission to interior Natives. It is uncertain, however, what Franciscan fathers would have received in return, except perhaps for a promise to allow for baptisms or to come to mass.

Beginning in the seventeenth century and extending into the mid-nineteenth century, glass "trade beads" were manufactured almost as a monopoly in the Bay of Venice on the Island of Murano. Although of European manufacture, these items ultimately became the possession of Native Americans.

While trade bead typologies are still in a state of flux, a generally accepted terminology has been applied to the presidio collection. In brief, the typology is based first on the method of manufacture (drawn, wound, mold-pressed, fired and blown), second on shape (rounded, chevron and faceted), then on color (typically blue, white, red and black) and lastly on decoration. Commonly, imported glass beads in the historic period have been called "trade beads" as a general term.

Because recent research has determined that at California mission and presidio sites glass beads were probably not always used to trade with Native people, the term "trade" will not be used. Instead, it is strongly suggested that glass beads were used as payment to Native workers rather than as vehicles of trade for goods or supplies. Also in California, and particularly on the frontier, these beads were also used by non-Native colonial occupants, most often by women as a decorative element of their dresses and shawls.

Based on an analysis of the beads from the Chapel Excavation, drawn beads were the most common and wound beads were second. This pattern is consistent with bead types discovered at Mission San Diego. There were

Blue faceted glass bead from the chapel excavation. *Author's collection.*

very few chevron-style beads; one was found in the housing/barracks area. Several of the more elaborate faceted beads were recovered in the Chapel Excavations.

At the San Diego Presidio, the priests, military personnel and artisans sometimes "traded" the beads to neophytes for material goods or for other Indigenous articles. Even more likely, beads may have been given as payment for labor, craftwork and as rewards for successful conversions. In addition to Commandant Rivera trading beads for fish, there is one other stark example. A soldier attempted to trade goods for sexual favors in 1775. Juan María Ruiz snuck out of the presidio after dark and visited a married Native woman at the nearby village of Kosaii. While her husband was tending to chores at a nearby corral, Ruiz offered the woman beads and cloth. She refused him, and when he heard her husband approaching, Ruiz fled back to the presidio. The guard on duty, José Antonio Peña, confiscated the illicit goods and turned them over to the mission priest. It is uncertain whether Ruiz was punished or not.

There were no attempts to apply the *reducciones*, or centralizing of Native inhabitants, in the mission or pueblos at San Diego. In part, this was because San Diego rarely produced enough food to feed a large captive population of neophytes. Also, by 1769, reducciones were falling into disfavor with Spanish officials. The labor situation at San Diego, at least, emerges as one of "forced communal labor" or bartered labor within which the Native people maintained and expressed agency. The Kumeyaay were recalcitrant people who constantly resisted authority. All these elements no doubt led to some Natives being compensated for their labor and artistic efforts, probably including payment in beads.

For instance, Native inhabitants at the presidio and at the mission were allowed, and encouraged, to go into the foothills and mountains during the early fall to hunt deer and rabbits and gather acorns and to the coast to fish. Such a movement would have allowed those neophytes who had earned or collected beads to trade or otherwise disseminate beads to Natives in the interior. If the neophyte in search of food entered an area controlled by clan members other than his own, he or she would have been expected to offer gifts. Relatively exotic glass beads would have been ideal. Reflective of this, glass beads have been found on archaeological sites in the inland valley and mountains.

The colors of beads represented in the presidio collection were predominantly blue or variations of blue (50 percent), white or variations of white (slightly more than 29 percent), green (almost 9 percent) and small percentages of black, yellow and clear. This data is consistent with percentages for beads at the San Diego Mission, a nearby Kumeyaay village (Micheagua) and at Mission San Gabriel, where, in all cases, blue beads were 50 percent or greater and, except at the presidio, white beads accounted for 18 percent or greater.

Top: White glass beads from the presidio chapel area. *Bottom*: Blue glass beads from the presidio chapel area. *Author's Collection.*

At the mission, black beads rather than white beads, at almost 29 percent, were the second most common color, and only 3 percent of the beads were white. This disparity among the black and white beads between the mission and the presidio may represent the ordering process at the presidio, where the military may have been in charge. Or the variation may reflect the Native population at the presidio, which had a higher percentage of non-local Native people and, thus, perhaps a differing preference of bead color.

Historical documents note that a variety of beads were brought along with Rivera as part of the overland expedition from Velicatá in Baja California to San Diego. On the same expedition, Gaspar de Portolá also transported beads. Colors given for some of the beads on that trek include milk white, blue and mixed. In the diaries of Portolá and others in his expedition north, they report dispensing glass beads at several coastal villages. Any beads that an official such as Rivera or Portolá might have possessed in the early colonial years separate from the shipments documented from San Blas to San Diego (and other locales) adds a level of possible bead types and colors, especially in more Indigenous, non-colonial contexts.

In contrast to what some scholars have suggested, trade between villages continued throughout the mission period. Consumption networks included shell and glass beads concurrently; the earlier traditional shell beads were not rejected automatically. One element of this trade may have been glass beads earned by workers and artisans at the mission and presidio and then traded to outlying villages. This is strongly suggested by glass beads at distant village sites such as Met Nuk in the eastern desert near Vallecitos over fifty miles from the mission and villages in the mountains that had minimal, if any, contact with the mission or presidio.

A view that Native people automatically embraced European goods because they were "superior" to precontact goods is probably inaccurate. A more accurate and culturally logical approach would be to understand that people accept those items that concur with their existing worldview and materialistic model. Acceptance and use of objects such as glass beads at the presidio and elsewhere need not be a sign of acculturation but rather of embracing a modification to traditional material types.

In the case of beads, the material from which they are made is perhaps not as relevant as their function and use. Shell and stone beads traditionally played a major role as funerary objects and carried spiritual significance. Augmenting such beads with colored glass beads does not reflect a shift in cosmology or eschatology. Glass beads recovered from Native burials at the presidio signify cultural continuity, not a cosmological shift.

The introduction and use of glass beads should also not be seen as completely replacing earlier shell beads. Shell beads continued to be manufactured and used in the historic period at Mission Santa Clara and elsewhere. At the San Diego mission, shell beads (primarily cupped sidewall and spire lopped *Olivella sp.* beads) were found in direct context with glass beads. While there may have been a reduction in the manufacture or importation of shell beads in the post-contact period, they continued as a cultural tradition. Accumulation of shell and glass beads through labor or trade offered symbols of status and wealth.

Trade items and exotic goods were accepted or rejected. Their incorporation into Native life was not automatic. In contrast to earlier assumptions, neophytes at the missions were not cut off from external colonial or Native trade (shells, cherts and obsidian). The presence of some colonial items such as glass beads does not reflect acculturation but rather improvising to existing patterns. This improvising, be it accepting glass beads or manufacturing arrow points from Spanish ceramics and glass, is internally structured and not just externally imposed. Native populations at the presidio, and at the mission, were their own active agents when it came to adoption of European goods.

It is important to know how the beads were gained and what the beads came to mean to Indigenous people. Beads of stone, wood and shell traditionally were incorporated into rituals and mourning. Precontact shell beads reflected status in several tribal burial contexts, and an augmentation, or partial replacement of shell beads by glass beads in burials, would be expected. One can imagine that after presidial graveside rites were completed and the priest stepped away, Native mourners would toss loose beads or strings of beads into the grave.

As noted by anthropologist Jerome Levi, for the Kumeyaay, east is identified with the color white (*nemeshap*), west with black (*nyilly*), north with red (*'ehwatt*) and south with blue or green (both designated by the same term, *hepeshiw*). The strong Kumeyaay correlation of colors and the cardinal directions in mythology and practice make the Kumeyaay one of the few California tribes to hold such a belief. Using information from song cycles, oral tradition and interviews, Levi suggests that the east (white) and south (blue green) represent more than cardinal directions on the land. As recorded by several researchers, the south (blue green) is the land of the dead, and Levi more specifically attaches that direction with the Sea of Cortez. Even so, Levi's suggestion that the south but also the east may be the Sea of Cortez, and the land of the dead is geographically accurate.

Applying Levi's color/cardinal direction/land of the dead concept to the mortuary beads at the presidio, one might expect a high percentage of blue and white beads in that context. As discussed above, blue and white glass beads composed 79.4 percent of all beads associated with burials. Assuming that cultural preference was a factor in the color of beads given to the presidial Native people, blue and white may have held significant meaning for the inhabitants. That would have been true when it came to burying the dead and ensuring their safe passage to the land of the dead.

Bead colors, especially blue and white, may also represent other underlying cultural symbols for the Natives. In Kumeyaay song and lore, blue can represent the sky and white the stars above us. Upon death, the Kumeyaay soul or spirit rises to the blue sky and travels among the white stars. Two major constellations, the Milky Way (Maay Hetat Kur) and the Northern Cross or Cygnus (Pehkaay/Pehkay), are ultimately traversed by human souls. This is after the soul has visited the four cardinal directions within the sky in search of shadows that it may have left behind.

For the Kumeyaay, Maay Hetaat Kur, the Milky Way, is perceived as the backbone of the sky and of the universe. Pehkaay (Northern Cross/ Cygnus) is a Kumeyaay word for "seven," perhaps referring to the number of stars composing the Cygnus constellation. Or it may denote the seven songs in the ilshaa funerary song cycle, or both. Crosses, or images that appear cross-like, predate the introduction of Christianity and appear in ancient rock art. Crosses may represent Cygnus, the constellation or the intersection of east–west and north–south directions. Taken together, the constellations of bright white stars and the blue sky itself may have been reflected in the blue and white beads placed in presidio (and mission) burials.

Artifacts Associated with Religion

Within the chapel itself, few items directly associated with religious practices were recovered except for, of course, the burials themselves and burial goods, usually crucifixes. One prominent find was a portion of the copper sheathing that once governed the communion rail at the altar. The approximately fifteen- to eighteen-foot-long copper sheathed rail separated the nave from the altar. In addition, Tonalá sherds from ceramic candelabras were recovered.

The Gateway Excavation produced at least ten small clappers from bells. Apparently, none were recorded at the chapel, although they may have been misidentified as earrings or other ornaments. The small bell

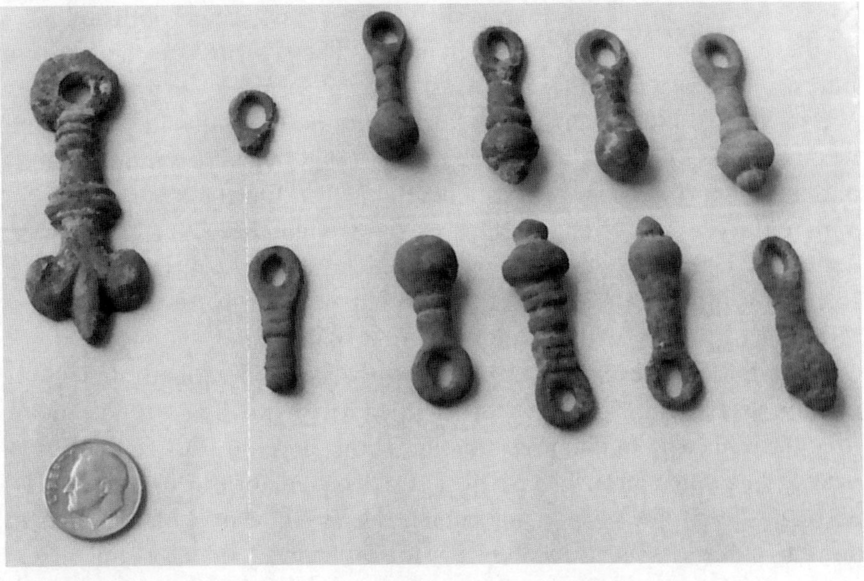

Metal bell clappers from the presidio Gateway Excavation. *Diane Everett Barbolla.*

clappers found at the gateway were cast rather than formed from sheet metal, which was common in some regions. They averaged from one inch to one and a half inches, with one large one shaped like a fleur-de-lis measuring two inches.

Such bells frequently served several purposes. Priests sometimes wore a small bell attached to a crucifix or necklace. A common belief was that the bells, or bells used as amulets, could ward off evil spirits and witches. A type of bell known as rumblers were used as hawk bells and fitted to children's toys and sewn onto clothing. Small bells were attached to children's clothing by way of a waist cord or string.

Early in the Dr. Brandes and Brockington excavations at the chapel, they recovered at least two clay figurines: one a head that they attributed to a saint and the other a full figure of what they called the Madonna. The "Saint's Head" showed substantial signs of wear on the nose and lips, which the archaeologists suggested was caused by devotees rubbing or touching the figure ritualistically.

Crucifixes

The crucifixes excavated from the chapel complex, burial ground and gateway trash pit all represent religious icons associated with followers of the Franciscan branch of Catholicism. These forms are the Latin or intersecting bar type and, in contrast to Jesuit forms, favor images of the Virgin Mary on the reverse. The Jesus figure on the front side commonly has the letters "INRI" above his head. He is lightly clothed in a loincloth, and a skull and crossbones rest beneath his feet. On the reverse side, the Virgin Mary is most often standing on a crescent moon with a halo of stars above her head. The seven stars are thought to represent the seven joys, sorrows or graces of Virgin Mary. The lack of Jesuit icons was expected, given the expulsion of the Jesuit order from Baja California in 1767.

In addition to several examples of the crucifix described above, one crucifix was a plain, unadorned, stamped lead type. This rustic crucifix may have been manufactured on site at the presidio. One crucifix is a heavily decorated bronze type of Jesus depicted on the front, "INRE" above his head. The reverse side depicts the Virgin Mary with folded arms and "B" above her head, a "VS" on the left arm of the cross and "PO" on the right arm; a "G" or "C" is below her feet. A third crucifix was also bronze with a fleur-de-lis on each arm of the cross and "INRE" inscribed

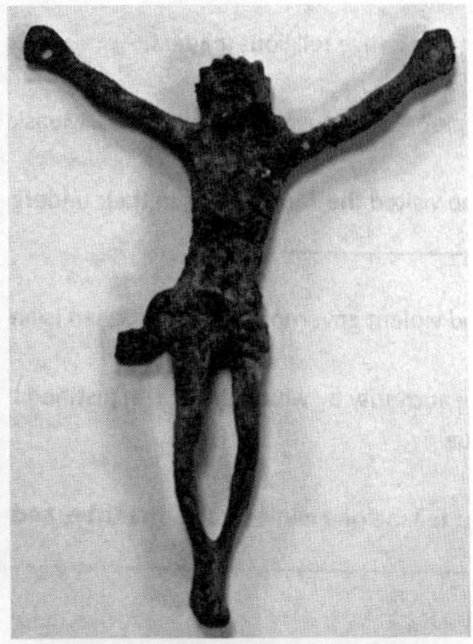

Above, left: Crucifix with Christ figure from Gateway Excavation. *Diane Everett Barbolla.*

Above, middle: Crucifix with Virgin Mary figure from Gateway Excavation. *Diane Everett Barbolla.*

Above, right: Christ figure with outstretched arms from Chapel Excavation. *Author's collection.*

Right: Floral-style cross from Gateway Excavation. *Diane Everett Barbolla.*

above the head. The reverse side is blank. A copper figure of Christ with outstretched arms was recovered at the chapel. As shown by the mounting holes in the figure's hands, this image was attached to a wooden cross or plaque. An unusual "floral" crucifix was recovered from the Gateway Excavation.

Other items associated with crucifixes include small metal chain links and both wooden and glass rosary beads. Many times, the rosary beads were strung on wire or metal links accompanying the crucifixes.

Medallions

Brass, copper and other metal medallions recovered at the presidio included mostly religious icons. These included medallions forged in honor of the Virgin Mary, a medallion commemorating the appearance of the Virgin Mary in Paris in 1830, a religious talisman known as "The Hand" and several others.

There are some artifacts that allow some chronological ordering, including the medallion discovered in association with an adult male (Burial 2). This medallion depicts the Virgin Mary on the front with her arms at her side astride a globe. The words "La Milagrosa de Paris" embellish the outer edges of the front, recalling the venerated 1830 Miracle of Paris, the Virgin Mary's appearance to Catherine Labouré, a novice in the Daughters of Charity.

Beginning in 1832, these medallions were struck by the tens of thousands and were worn and cherished by both men and women. There are at least two versions of the medal. The first is the version described to Saint Catherine by the Virgin Mary, with instructions to have them manufactured in her honor. According to Catherine, the Virgin Mary thought that the people of Paris were falling away from the Catholic Church. She told Catherine that the medal would remind them of her and of the one true God.

A second commemorates the event itself and differs from the style initially told to Saint Catherine and includes the date of 1830 at the base. The medals recovered at the presidio chapel are of both types. The example from the gateway is of the second type.

A similar medallion carrying the raised date of 1830 (the date of the miracle, not of manufacture) on the bottom of the piece was found in what is assumed to be the priests' quarters east of the sanctuary. This location was near Burial 23, a possible Native American burial from the 1870s, although it may not be associated. By inference then, Burial 2 and possibly Burial 23 were interred sometime after approximately 1832.

One medallion found in the gateway trash pits had been partially severed on the left side. Whether the severing of the medal was to get the brass or to defile the medal is not known. The Miracle of Paris medallion appears in archaeological contexts from St. Augustine, Florida, to California and serves not only as a religious icon but also as a reliable chronological marker.

A single *higa*, or fist-shaped metal amulet known as "The Hand," was recovered in the general area of disturbed burials within the campo santo but is, unfortunately, lacking accurate provenience. Higas are amulets made

Top, left: Miracle of Paris 1830 medallion from Chapel Excavation. *Author's collection.*

Top, right: Miracle of Paris medallion, no date, Gateway Excavation. The left side is cut off. *Diane Everett Barbolla.*

Bottom: Religious talisman. *La higa*: the hand. From the Chapel Excavation. *Author's collection.*

of jet in the early Spanish colonial period and of glass and metal in later years. Higas are associated with folk superstition and magic rather than more doctrinaire religion. With the thumb protruding between the index finger and middle fingers of a fist, these objects were used to ward or fight off the *mal de ojo*, or evil eye. While not approved or sanctioned by the Catholic Church, higas persisted throughout the Spanish Empire with special powers to protect young children.

Personal Items

A few rings were recorded from the Chapel Excavations. Most of these were found in the context of burials and included rings of bone, wood and metal. The metal rings were made of copper, silver and gold. Most metal rings were simple bands, although there were at least two rings that had unrecognizable emblems. One ring had Chinese inscriptions. Another ring had inset turquoise glass. Several sets of possible cuff links were recovered in association with burials. These items may also have been small bell clappers or earrings. A dart brooch that would have been worn as a decorative ornament was recovered. In the case of the earrings and brooch, their condition was too degraded to discern decorative designs or symbols.

A variety of coins were found, although most of these were modern coins (1945–60) and reflect coins lost at the site over the years. The exception to this was a Spanish coin dated 1777. The silver coin is an eight reales piece bearing an image of King Carlos III on the front and the Latin words *Dei Gratia*, meaning "By the Grace of God." Other metal items included watch parts, thimbles, copper braid, tinklers and broken knife blades.

Clay pipe stems were recovered from the refuse area near the chapel. One had been painted green and white. No obvious pipe bowls were recovered. Both wooden and bone combs or comb fragments were found. A crochet

Opposite, top: Spanish eight reales coin from 1777 from Chapel Excavation. King Carlos is on the front side. *Author's collection.*

Opposite, bottom: King Carlos III depicted on the front side of a Spanish eight reales coin from 1777. *Author's collection.*

Above: Silver banded turquoise ring from Chapel Excavation. *Author's collection.*

hook found at the site shows manufacture or repair of woven items. As would be expected given decades of irrigation and application of fertilizer to the soil and sod overburden, only minimal clothing or cloth was recovered, most of it within the cemetery area. There were fragmentary examples of braiding, sequins, leather belts and belt buckles and lace.

Buttons reflecting primarily military types and, to a lesser extent, ordinary civilian types were recovered. Most of these were within the upper modern levels of the site. Older buttons were found in association with burials, from the refuse dump, from the barracks area and essentially throughout the presidio. Most nonmilitary buttons were manufactured from wood, shell, glass or bone. Buttonholes, when they occurred, varied from two-hole to four-hole.

The few military buttons were copper or brass with shanks rather than holes for attachment. Burial 3, a male interred within the chapel, was tentatively identified as a sailor based on his maritime-style buttons. These brass or copper buttons were of a domed style, with a rope coiled around an anchor. They would have been attached to his uniform with a shank that secured the thread.

One of the more intriguing button types recovered is the so-called phoenix button. These brass disk buttons were manufactured in England for the troops of King Henri Christophe of Haiti, who emulated Napoleon's armies. Dates of manufacture have been suggested as sometime between 1812 and 1830. However, the date is more likely 1822 given the fact that King Christophe committed suicide in October 1820 and his successors sold off the court goods shortly after. Once thought to be rare in Southern California, phoenix buttons are ubiquitous by their presence, if not frequency, at mission period sites and at late contact period sites.

It appears that thousands of phoenix buttons were purchased in Haiti by seafaring traders, including Nathaniel Wyeth, and sold to both Native Americans and European settlers in the New World, especially in the Pacific Northwest, sometime after 1820. Precisely how hundreds, if not thousands, of English-made, Haitian military buttons came to the Pacific Coast is uncertain. Most probably, introducing phoenix buttons in Spanish colonial or Californio San Diego was through direct trade between the Yankee traders and residents rather than through secondary trade out of the Pacific Northwest. The buttons may have come in with English ceramics and other goods from England and Europe in the early 1820s.

Distribution of phoenix buttons in California has generally been restricted to mission sites or military posts, although their presence in contact period Indian sites is also well documented. Excavations at California mission sites at San Antonio de Padua, San Juan Capistrano, Santa Barbara, San Buenaventura, Santa Ynez, Carmel, San Luis Rey and Mission San Diego have all produced phoenix buttons.

Phoenix buttons were produced in two different sizes and three different styles of bird designs. Each button portrays a legendary phoenix bird rising from a fringe of flames with the motto *Je Renais de Mes Cendres* ("I am reborn from my ashes") in raised letters around the outer button edge. Individual regiment numbers (1 through 9, 10, 14, 20 and 25 through 30) appear below the phoenix. Regiment numbers 1, 8, 25, 29 and 30 were recovered at the presidio chapel and cemetery. At the gateway excavation, Regiments 4, 5, 6, 7, 20, 26, 27, 28 and 30 were recovered.

Regiment 25 phoenix button from the Chapel Excavation. *Author's collection.*

By contrast, excavation at the San Diego mission turned up only Regiments 4, 5, 9 and 27, with only 5 being common to both facilities. Because neither the mission nor the presidio has been completely excavated, the actual presence or absence of certain regiments may be biased. It is unlikely that the phoenix buttons were worn by soldiers at the presidio. Instead, they may have been sewn onto clothing, used as gaming pieces or strung by their shanks as necklaces.

Artifacts themselves form the backbone of most archaeological studies, but special studies can also play a major role in understanding the past. Because the excavations at the presidio took place before the advancement of DNA studies and other amazing scientific methods, special studies at the site were limited. One study that was attempted was to X-ray metal objects such as medallions and crucifixes that were heavily encrusted with rust. The advantage of using radiology instead of chemical cleaners is that X-ray analysis is nondestructive.

Dr. David Adams, a local private radiologist and the father of the student excavator Therese Adams, agreed to conduct a series of X-rays on metal objects recovered from the presidio. Results of the X-rays were mixed depending on the type of metal and corrosion. One example of a medallion found by Ellen Lennert produced usable results. The oval-shaped medallion was discovered to be one of the Miracle of Paris icons minted after 1830. Besides allowing researchers to categorize the type of medallion, the study provided an approximate date for the deposit in which it was uncovered.

Soil samples were taken from selected locations to better understand the soil types and their deposition within the site. These samples are still curated by the university and may yet produce information on the acidity and alkalinity of the soils and could, in rare cases of soils from the cemetery, provide organic material for DNA studies. Obsidian, a black volcanic rock used by Native people for arrow points and cutting tools, was found at the site. Visually, the samples appeared to be from a well-known source called Obsidian Butte more than one hundred miles east of the presidio. It is also possible that the glassy samples are from sources in Baja California. In the future, nondestructive X-ray fluorescence (XRF) studies may verify the source of the presidio obsidian. Chemical and visual studies on shellfish samples could determine the season of their capture and even the water temperature at the time, thus contributing to climate change studies.

Chapter 13

PRESIDIAL CUISINE

From Carne Asada to Tortillas

One of the questions that careful archaeological excavation can answer is what were the people at this site eating? How did they prepare their food? Over the seven decades that the presidio was occupied, food habits and diet went through some changes. For instance, cattle, pigs and sheep would have been rare in the early years, as both the presidio and the mission struggled to raise herds of livestock. Mission San Gabriel, established in 1771, was highly successful in raising cattle, and by 1778, herds of cattle were driven from that mission to San Diego. Ultimately, San Diego had hundreds of head of livestock, including sheep for wool.

Until presidial herds were established, the colonists focused on chicken, fish, shellfish, deer and rabbits for their protein. Overall, a distinctly Mexican-Californio cuisine dominated the dining tables at the presidio. It is also possible that acorn gruel, produced by Kumeyaay women, may have been eaten. Two important foods, corn and flour tortillas, were constant throughout the years. Lacking refrigeration, most of the more perishable foods would have been jerked, smoked or salted.

Cooking techniques favored meats that were axed or cleaved rather than the European methods of sawing, slicing and butchering an animal into distinct cuts, such as chops or filets. In general, meat was reduced to small pieces, to include in soups and stews, rather than served as steaks. Marinaded and seared pieces of meat known as carne asada would have been popular. Roasting in earth ovens and boiling were typical cooking techniques for larger cuts, including whole animal heads. Some of the larger cattle bones had clearly been split to extract the marrow.

The frontier diet included beef, wild birds, deer, ducks, pork, jackrabbits, chickens and, on rare occasions, turkey. At least twenty avian species were identified in a sample study conducted by the San Diego Zooarchaeology Laboratory at the San Diego Natural History Museum. Chicken proved to be the dominant avian species and in far greater numbers than reported thus far at Alta California's missions and presidios. Two types of chicken were defined from archaeological studies: a bantam and a regular-sized fowl.

The chickens would have been raised by the soldiers' wives, their children and perhaps other women working at the presidio. Approximately 75 percent of the chicken bone came from the west wing excavations in and around the presidio residential units. This concentration makes sense given that this was the most densely occupied area. Roasting was the most common method of preparing the chickens. Butchering, except for disjointing by knife or cleaver, was minimal. In addition to meat, the flock would also have provided eggs and feathers.

The data provided by archaeological excavation and study by the Zooarchaeology Laboratory offer glimpses into presidio life absent in the historical records. When compared to cows, pigs and sheep, chickens are rarely mentioned in mission and presidial inventories. Husbandry based on cattle and sheep gets most of the attention. The underrepresentation of chicken husbandry in the historical record is another sign that women's roles at the presidio were taken for granted or, sometimes, ignored.

The coastal waters and lagoons offered a variety of shellfish, including abalone, mussels and clams. Deer and antelope (no longer present in the region) were common in the foothills and mountains of San Diego. While there is little documentation that the soldiers or others at the presidio fished the nearby waters, Native fishermen no doubt supplied the bass, tuna, eels, sardines, halibut, barracuda and other marine life found in the archaeological deposits.

Diaries and memoirs of the period noted Kumeyaay canoes and fishing craft. Kumeyaay fishermen were not content to fish just in the offshore kelp beds. They ventured out into deeper water in search of larger fish species. While not conclusive, it appears that in many cases, the fish were gutted, cleaned and then smoked or dried before being brought back to the presidio. Presidial children may have contributed to meals through clamming along San Diego and False (Mission) Bay.

Native plants such as cactus pods were roasted, and cactus fruit (called tuna) provided a sweet delicacy. Onions, both native wild varieties and introduced types, were used, as well as a wide variety of red and green chiles, squash and watermelons. Once milk cows were introduced, cheeses were produced, both fresh cheese and cheeses for aging. As with many Hispanic cultures, milk was not commonly served as a beverage; it was more typically made into cheeses, allowed to sour to make crema fresca or incorporated into recipes. Inventories for the San Diego Mission show that once herds of cattle and sheep were viable, several pounds of cheese were made on a regular basis. The presidio probably had its own cheesemakers.

A common beverage was agua fresca, a refreshing drink made from fruit pulp, seeds or grains. The settlement was not without its alcoholic beverages either. Grapes from the vineyards at the nearby mission were fermented into a low-alcohol wine that was described as thin but drinkable. For more potency, a fortified wine beverage, *aguardiente*, was produced. Aguardiente resembles brandy and was the drink of choice for special occasions and at the frequent card games in the barracks. In contrast to the low alcohol level in wine (about 12 percent), aguardiente could run from 30 percent to as high as 60 percent. Tea, coffee and cacao rounded out the beverage choices on Presidio Hill. The tea could be from local plants such as elderberry, ephedra and Yerba Buena or, if one could afford it, from China. Chinese tea shipped to California or to California by way of Mexico arrived in compressed blocks rather than as loose tea leaves.

Coffee beans were brought up from San Blas and roasted and then ground fresh. To stretch the amount, other seeds or grains were added to the beverage. Some accounts note native chia would be added to ground coffee. If cinnamon was available, it was added to sugared coffee to make café de olla, still a common breakfast drink in parts of Mexico. Chocolate from the cacao bean imported into the area was commonly made with water rather than milk, to which sugar was added. Chocolate was considered an essential food item and not necessarily a luxury. The San Diego Mission employed a Native man as a chocolatier. It is also possible that Kumeyaay beverages were drunk at the presidio, including those made from lemonade berry, manzanita or sugar bush.

The water for all cooking and beverages had to be brought up from wells or, during seasonal flows, the San Diego River. At one time, a spring-fed pond of water existed in a canyon bottom below the presidio and to the east. The larger Tizon brown ware ollas holding at least five gallons were used specifically for water storage. Botijas may have also been used.

Given San Diego's temperate semi-arid climate, most of the cooking would have been done outside of the homes and military quarters. There is no evidence that there was a regular mess hall or military kitchen. Instead, the wives of married men cooked for their immediate family but also pitched in to cook for the single men, including the clergy when they visited on Sundays or for burials. Community ovens known as *hornos* or *estufas* were shared by families, thus reducing the need for scarce firewood.

A large horno behind the chapel in the common courtyard area may also have been shared. Smaller communal ovens in the yards behind the casitas must have existed. For fresh vegetables, families would have had their own small gardens or shared a community garden. Native plants such as cactus, chia, yucca flowers and buckwheat may have been integrated into the presidial diet.

Closely associated with plant foods, certain of the Native women at the presidio would have known the medicinal qualities of native plants. The wide variety of plants available from the nearby marshlands, the riverside and the deep canyons could provide food and medicines. Ephedra, besides being a tea, could aid in cleaning the kidneys. Ailments of the eyes could be treated with swamp root (*yerba mansa*), and willow bark steeped in water reduced headaches. White sage served several purposes, including as a medicinal tea, as a salve to treat wounds and chest colds and, when burnt, to purify a room.

There were sporadic food shortages, especially in the early years of the presidio, 1769–78, and in the later years in the lead-up to the Mexican revolution and afterward. In 1821, presidio officials pleaded with the priests at several missions to supply seeds and grains to the garrison. They reported that tortillas and beans were in especially short supply. They also noted that not only had intense rainfall spoiled crops at the San Diego Mission intended for the presidio but also the roads became impassable to obtain supplies from the north. Lard from Mission San Gabriel that was allotted to the presidio could not be transported one season because of the poor condition of the rain-soaked El Camino Royal. Such were the vagaries of transportation and internal shipping in Southern California. Instead, it was turned into soap before it spoiled.

Chapter 14

GAMES, MUSIC, SPORTS AND LEISURE TIME

Archaeological excavation produced information on otherwise poorly documented activities at the presidio. Military life on the frontier could be tedious and boring, but there were always outlets for adults and children alike. No doubt the record is incomplete given that many types of toys and games were made from perishable items and would have vanished long ago. The Native people at the presidio may have introduced traditional games such as stick dice, the lance and hoop game, shooting arrows at a target on the ground (which may explain some of the arrow points on the site) and various games of chance.

There are historic accounts of presidial soldiers gambling and playing monte. Allegedly, soldiers would sneak down from the presidio to Canon de Diablo (Devil's Canyon), historically also called Pumphouse Canyon, to play monte. There, they would bet their meager wages trying to guess matching suits of cards. In the early to mid-1800s, monte was essentially the Mexican national card game. This form of monte spread into the American West and is often portrayed in western movies. Mexican monte is not to be confused with the three-card version, which is essentially a con game.

Examples of artifacts found at the presidio reflecting children's toys and games included a small three-inch-long clay cannon and two cannonballs. Both clay and glass marbles were also found. Two ceramic animals made from Tonalá were recovered and may have been toys or perhaps decorative figurines. Pieces of slate and nubs of chalk recovered at the presidio may be associated with the school taught at one time by Manuel Vargas. Small slate tablets were used for students to write on and do math problems.

Mexican monte card game on the streets of Mexico City. *Amon Carter Museum of American Art.*

Two small discs, one of Tizon brown ware and one of undecorated pearl ware, were also recovered. At other sites, these have been labeled as two-sided dice, counting devices/chips or small lids. Toys that may have been used by presidial children but perished include cloth dolls and small burros made from corn husks, crepe paper animals and wooden dice. Popular toys of the period not found intact at the presidio were small wheeled dragons. It is possible that fragments of miniature metal and wooden wheels that were discovered came from those or similar popular toys.

Although artifacts associated with musical instruments are rare so far in the presidio collections, when Williams's collection from the barracks is analyzed, that picture may change. A single whole harmonica has been noted, and some fragments of guitar bridge parts and tuning pegs may reflect musical elements. While singing, especially of the "Ave Maria" and of plainsongs (chants), was probably the most common music, guitar music may have resonated off the adobe walls of the church and the barracks. Certainly, most accounts of barracks life and campsites mention guitar music and the occasional harmonica. Mexican folk music, later formed as ever-popular *corridos*, would have been sung. Popular topics would have been lost love, gunfights, ranch life and longing for home.

Two activities that did not show up in the archaeological record but are documented in the literature deserve special attention. Both may have started as elements of sport but ultimately led to faunal remains. One sport the soldiers engaged in was to place an old hen or rooster in a shallow pit on the parade grounds with only the neck and head above ground. Then, adept horsemen would ride past the chicken and try to strike the hapless creature with a curved stick resembling a hockey stick. The ideal strike would behead the chicken (thus the bird's potential to end up in the faunal remains category). It could, however, take several strikes to dispatch or behead the bird. This sport is still practiced in some rural areas of Mexico, and intense betting is often part of the event.

On a much larger scale, a bull from the herd would occasionally be brought to the enclosed parade grounds and chased by men with capes or cloth. Not truly a bullfight, it was more of a show of bravado involving a no doubt bewildered bull. In one recorded instance, probably after 1783, a bull ran away from the harassers, charged up the hill to the east and then made a sharp right, which brought it level with the rear roof of the chapel. The bull proceeded to run west along the tiled roof until it fell through the roof and into the nave. Soldiers were sent into the church to extract the injured and stunned animal. Carne asada or beef burritos may have been on the menu shortly thereafter.

Chapter 15

CRIME AND PUNISHMENT AT THE PRESIDIO

The presidio was always more than a military base; it also served as an administrative institution for the region. The commandant or ranking military officer had certain judicial authority over his men and, most times, over the Native people. Priests, at least ostensibly, had the authority to punish Native transgressors for crimes against the Church. But the military retained authority in secular affairs. For criminal cases, a set of legal regulations dictated that alleged perpetrators (both Native and Spaniard/Californio) be given a hearing before a panel of officers. Because San Diego lacked civil authorities, the panel was composed of military officials. The defendant was given at least some level of legal defense in the form of a person who was at least familiar with the law. Sometimes, an officer from another presidio would be brought in. Consistent with Spanish protocol, a detailed record of the proceedings was transcribed.

While awaiting trial, alleged criminals were imprisoned in the presidio jail on the west side of the presidio. The cells were small, squat and often described as cage-like. In 1820, Father José Sanchez complained to the governor that two Native vaqueros were being held in the presidio prison for no good cause. Sanchez reported that their only crime was reporting a presidio soldier in the backcountry with a Kumeyaay woman who had run away from the mission. The outcome of this event is uncertain, but it reflects Father Sanchez's concern, even if only for procedural reasons.

In another instance, a priest visiting the presidio reported that a Kumeyaay prisoner had been severely cut by a prolonged whipping. He wrote that maggots were crawling from the prisoner's wounds. The prisoner later died. Spanish regulations stated a prisoner could only be given forty *azotes* (lashes) per day. Further, the lashings were to be administered with a broad strap, not a thin or sharp-edged leather that would cut. Those edicts were clearly not always enforced.

Relations between the Native population and the presidial forces occasionally took a tragic turn. Before his murder in November 1775, Father Luis Jayme complained to the viceroy of rapes of Native women. A particular atrocity took place at the presidio corrals near present-day El Cajon. Jayme documented one rape and a gang rape of another Tipai young woman.

In another case, while walking from her village at Rincon de Jamo (at present-day Pacific Beach), a nearly blind Iipai woman was assaulted by three soldiers. In testimony, the rapists' names were given as José Rafael Hernandez, José Marcelino Bravo and Julian Murillo. She struggled, but to no avail; the men raped her and left her in the dirt alongside the trail to the mission/presidio. The unfortunate woman became pregnant from the ordeal. Following traditional protocol, the tribe refused to allow the child to live. For Bravo, this was the second time he was accused of rape. Despite protests by tribal members and the clergy, the soldiers were simply transferred to another presidio.

In other cases, Native men and soldiers convicted of serious crimes were sentenced to years of labor and served their time in the prison. The forced labor could be either common or hard labor. Some, to increase the severity of crimes committed by Native men, were exiled to separate them from their families and culture.

Three Iipay men—Fermin, Francisco and Fernando—were convicted of murdering a *majordomo* (an administrator or overseer) at a sheep camp in the Ballena Valley near Ramona. After a lengthy hearing and even a visit to the crime scene, the men received ten-year sentences of labor at the presidio. This sentence was given only after they were first sentenced to be hanged and then dismembered.

Upon appeal, their public defender, José de la Guerra, briefly the commandant of the San Diego Presidio and later the commandant of the Santa Barbara Presidio, pleaded their case. He claimed that the deceased majordomo had carnal relations with Fermin's wife and had unjustly whipped the three men. He also argued they did not clearly understand the

Spanish legal system. Guerra was cleverly using the Spaniards' belief that Native people were like children against the prosecutor. The panel lessened the sentence to imprisonment without exile.

The men began their sentences in February 1826 and reportedly did public works within the presidio walls. Later, the men reported to the governor that they suffered in the presidio prison. They said that their cell was a cage that did not shelter them from the icy winds. They also lamented that their meals were nothing more than *atole* (corn gruel) that they described as colored water. Their families could not bring them food or clothing. Despite their repeated pleas to the viceroy and the governor for clemency, these men may have only been released in 1835 when the presidio troops left the decaying fort.

The three convicted murderers shared their prison, although not their cells, with Sylvester Pattie, an American fur trapper. Pattie, his son James Ohio and several other men turned themselves in to Commandant José María Echeandía in late March 1828. The men had spent months in the American Southwest and endured several skirmishes with Native Americans. They were possibly the first American trappers to make a western trek south of the Sierra Nevadas by way of New Mexico and Arizona. When they arrived at the presidio, they presented letters of safe passage from authorities in New Mexico.

But less than a decade after Mexican independence, Echeandía believed the men to be spies for the Spanish government and imprisoned them. A prideful man, Echeandía told the Americans that he was the authority for all of California. He cared little for what someone in New Mexico might have written.

In his somewhat fanciful memoir, James Pattie wrote that from the barred window of his prison cell, he could see Echeandía out on his patio. Pattie lamented that if he had his trusty long rifle, he could have easily dispatched the treacherous Mexican governor. Pattie had more favorable words for an unidentified woman and a soldier. He wrote that she brought him tortillas and other food to supplement his otherwise meager food ration. The soldier also treated him kindly.

Less than one month after the trappers' imprisonment, Sylvester Pattie, who had been ill for several months, died of unstated causes in his solitary prison cell. His son wrote later that his father was buried outside the presidio walls. Later, James Pattie served as an interpreter for Echeandía when American ships or travelers visited San Diego. Pattie was released by Echeandía in 1829, one year after his imprisonment. In a published memoir, James Ohio Pattie claimed that after his release, he treated thousands of Californios for smallpox. Most historians believe his boast is exaggerated given that the smallpox epidemic occurred before the Patties arrived in Southern California and that the disease of 1829–30 was measles, not smallpox.

Chapter 16

SUMMARY AND CONCLUSIONS

After decades of archaeological excavation, extensive research on Spanish and Mexican documents and analysis of literally tens of thousands of artifacts, a fuller story of the San Diego Presidio has emerged from the mists of time. As Spain's first outpost in upper California, the story of the presidio and its people is a vital piece of history. It was more than a fort, more than Alta California's first mission and far more than its less than seventy years of occupation might show. The presidio was a diverse frontier community, first Spanish and then Mexican/Californio. In so many ways (economic, political, social and cultural), the presidio reflected decades of change and growth.

It was, of course, where the first Franciscan mission north of Baja California was founded in 1769 by Junípero Serra. There would be twenty more missions in upper California, but San Diego was the first. From its tenuous hold on that dusty sage-covered hillside, the roots of Spain's northern empire spread even farther north. The first of Alta California's twenty-one missions and four presidios, the tenacious settlement housed soldiers, artisans, wives, Native workers and, sometimes, prisoners.

Erase any thoughts you might have about metal-helmeted conquistadors, soldiers in matching colorful uniforms or purebred Spaniards living within the adobe walls. Except for the small contingent of Catalonian soldiers from Spain, few presidial occupants had ever set foot in Europe. Their homeland was in the New World, in the ever-expanding Spanish empire.

The presidio housed mestizos from the interior of Mexico and Baja California and Afro-Caribbeans from Cuba within the presidio confines. Native people from the local Kumeyaay tribes, the Cochimi of Baja California and from the Colorado River region also lived and died on Presidio Hill. Sometimes they lived as prisoners, indentured servants or military wives. The clothing they wore and the languages they spoke bore witness to their diversity.

As expected, the presidio housed not only soldiers but also their wives and children. In fact, the total number of wives and children outnumbered the soldiers in the later years of the presidio. The recovered artifacts and food remains paint a picture of a class of people in the middle of Spanish and then the Californio economic and cultural spectrum. Lacking steady supplies from mainland Mexico, these people had to be at least partially self-sufficient. The carpenters and blacksmiths played a major role in repairing and sometimes manufacturing the tools and implements needed to survive on the Spanish and, later, Mexican frontier. Native Kumeyaay women supplied the presidio with a variety of ceramic vessels for cooking and serving meals.

The priests and officers, of course, probably ate better, sipped quality wine more often and ate their meals off more costly table settings. Their clothes may have been cleaner and in better repair than the average soldier or artisan, but probably not by much. After the Mexican revolution and the opening of less restrictive trade in the 1820s, the occupants of the presidio gained access to more foreign goods, including those from China, England and France. Globalization is hardly new; it had its roots many years ago. The San Diego Presidio was not a closed-economic system; it was open to the world.

Death came to the people of the presidio in a variety of ways. Soldiers died from arrows shot into them by Kumeyaay rebels. Kumeyaay men hanged themselves, died by execution and passed from unknown causes in the dank presidio prison. Spanish and Californio children and their mothers died from diseases, especially in years that witnessed epidemics, such as 1826–27. Some children, and perhaps their mothers, probably died at birth. In death, most found their ultimate resting place in consecrated ground within and outside the presidio chapel. But then there were others—Native rebels, an American fur trapper and non-Catholics—who lie in the soil beyond consecrated ground.

The presidio saw its share of well-known historical figures, including Junípero Serra, Juan Bautista Anza, Fernando Rivera y Moncada and other notable men of the Spanish colonization. There were also the less well known, but no less important to their families and friends. This included Native people such as brave Kumeyaay rebels like Naguasajo, Native women who married into Spanish culture and mixed-race children of those marriages who formed the basis for multi-ethnic, multicultural Southern California. Prominent Californio families associated with the presidio include the Carrillos, the Osunas, the Ruizs, the Silvas, the Marrons and several others.

Chapter 17

THE PRESIDIO DE SAN DIEGO TODAY

Various groups such as the San Diego History Center, the Save Our Heritage Organisation and the Old Town Descendants Group keep the memory of Alta California's first settlement and its people alive. They know well that more than 250 years of history lay buried there. For them, Presidio Hill is more than a place. It is a repository of history, a buried storybook of lives and deaths. It marks the beginning and end of historic eras.

These groups rightfully believe that the presidio is a landmark with a unique story to tell. Presidio Hill is listed on the National Register of Historic Places and is a listed state and city landmark. The History Center staffs the architecturally important Serra Museum on weekends, and there are occasional guided tours sponsored by different groups. Displays and mixed media within the museum tell the story of Alta California's first mission and settlement. Once lost and forgotten, the original saints' statues that once sat in the chapel's niches are now housed at Mission San Luis Rey, located thirty-five miles north of Presidio Hill.

Nestled on a hill above Old Town San Diego, Presidio Park gets far less human traffic and tourists than the popular State Park below. It is, however, the scene of picnics and weddings. Thousands of tourists, both local and distant, do the trek up to the Serra Museum (on weekends) to view the exhibits. It is a hike up to the museum because parking can be limited and there is no direct route to stroll up to the site from Old Town.

Mexican Soldado, circa 1830, as depicted by Italian painter Claudio Linati. *Amon Carter Museum of American Art.*

From the parking lot, visitors can walk over to the south and see the recreated bastion that sits in the approximate location that it held in the late 1700s. Because of a pentagram installed by the San Diego Chapter of the United States Daughters of 1812, the bastion has been given the name "Witches Tower." Local paranormal groups foster the idea that the park is haunted by Lucy, a white deer that, when alive, roamed the park for many years; a robed monk; and other phantoms from the past. Occasionally, the bastion is one stop on special Halloween tours of the area.

On one wall of the bastion is a plaque dedicated to the intrepid but ill-fated American trapper Sylvester Pattie. The plaque describes Pattie as the first American buried in Mexican California soil. He is, in fact, buried there somewhere under the sod and irrigation system that keeps the park green. Perhaps he is one of the restless spirits who roam the ancient ruins.

If visitors venture down below the Order of Panama Serra Cross and veer to the south a bit, they will see the undulating mounds that mark the melted walls of Alta California's first Catholic church. Next to those mounds is the cemetery where over two hundred early pioneers and Native people rest. If visitors look closely at the arrangement of the mounds and select the largest north–south wall and walk there, they will be standing above the chapel's altar. In recent years, couples have been married right there. Above the incessant traffic noise from the nearby I-8 and I-5 freeways, maybe a faint "Ave Maria" melody can be heard or the sobs of a loved one mourning one of the hundreds of people buried there in the old cemetery.

Should a visitor wander across the two-lane paved road and head north or west, they will be in the quadrant that held the troops' quarters, guardhouse, prison and gateway. With a good imagination, they might hear some Spanish charros being played on a slightly out-of-tune guitar. Perhaps the smell of fresh tortillas will rise from the buried ovens or the aroma of a hearty guisado (stew) of pork, cilantro and onions will waft by. Maybe the smoke from one of the dark, acrid cigars so prized by the soldiers can be sensed. If a spirit wants to play monte with you, you might want to keep walking.

Should our visitors go to the west and brave the traffic barreling around the blind corner, they can stand on the outer edge of the presidio itself. It may be here, just beyond the wall, that Sylvester Pattie lies in his grave. To the south was the prison where Kumeyaay men suffered and died. Farther west, at the base of the hill, is where Father Serra supposedly planted California's first nonnative palm. A garden planted by presidial families also once existed there.

In the center was the gateway where sailors, troops and weary travelers made their way up the hill, across the parade grounds and plaza to the door of the commanding officer. Occasionally, Kumeyaay prisoners or presidial soldiers were fastened to stockades and whipped in that plaza. From the platform that holds the massive adobe Serra tile cross, visitors can look out over Mission Bay, once called False Bay. Looking to the south, they might glimpse San Diego Bay and Point Loma, where the supply ships anchored, although not frequently enough.

Presidio Hill still holds many of its secrets. Those probing archaeologists left plenty of discoveries for future generations. But for now, there is no reason to dig any further. There are tens of thousands of uncatalogued and unanalyzed artifacts to pore over. Dusty documents in the archives in Mexico City, Madrid and California await translation and interpretation. Incomplete chapters of the story of life and death on Presidio Hill have been told, but far more await storytellers who know there is so much yet to tell.

GLOSSARY

ADOBE: Can be a type of clay soil or fired and unfired bricks and tiles of that soil

AGUARDIENTE: A brandy-like beverage made at most California missions from grapes

ALFEREZ: A captain in the military

AZOTE: A lash administered by a whip or rawhide strip

BALDOSAS: A term applied regionally to fired adobe tiles; see also ladrillo

CALIFORNIO: A person of Spanish or Mexican ethnicity and heritage living in Alta California in the first decades of the 1800s and identified more as a resident of California than as a citizen of Mexico

CAMPO SANTO: Literally, resting place of saints; a cemetery

COLOR QUEBRADO: A person of mixed ancestry and/or bloodlines

COYOTE: A person who was described as part mestizo and part Native

ESTUFA: A type of stove or brazier

GENTE DE RAZON: Literally, people of reason; applied to non-Indigenous colonists

GENTILE: An unconverted Native person

HORNO: An oven either for firing clay or for baking/cooking

KWAAPAAY: One of several leaders in Kumeyaay settlements; often a political leader

LADRILLO: A kiln-fired clay brick or tile; also called baldosas

LAVANDERÍA: A tiled area supplied with water where clothing was washed or cleansed

MAIOLICA: Common glazed ceramics produced in the interior of Mexico; also spelled Majolica and Mayolica

MESTIZO: A person of mixed Spanish/Mexican bloodlines and Native/Indigenous bloodlines

MULATTO: An ethnic term now considered inappropriate but used in the eighteenth century (and beyond) to describe a person of African and Spanish/Mexican bloodlines

NEOPHYTE: A Native person who has been baptized and had communion

POBRE CHOZA: A basic reed hut

TEJAS: Curved fired adobe clay roof tiles

TIZON BROWN WARE: Unglazed Native ceramic ware specific to the San Diego region

TONALÁ: Ancient form of Mexican ceramic, modified by Spanish artisans, that has burnishing and is typically painted with animals and other figures

VARA: A unit of Spanish measurement; although variable throughout the land, one vara in San Diego typically equaled thirty-three inches

BIBLIOGRAPHY

Axtell, James. "Some Thoughts on the Ethnohistory of Missions." *Ethnohistory* 29, no. 1 (1982): 35–41.

Bancroft, Hubert H. *History of California*. A.L. Bancroft Co., 1884.

Barbolla, Diane Everett. "Alta California Troops: Acculturation and Material Wealth in a Presidio and Mission Context, 1769–1810." Dissertation on file at the University of California–Riverside, 1992.

———. "Maiolica at the San Diego Presidio Gateway Research Project." *Journal of San Diego History* 29, no. 3 (1983).

Bartel, Brad. "Archaeological Excavation and Education at the San Diego Royal Presidio, 1987–1990." *Journal of San Diego History* 37, no. 4 (1991).

Benté, Vance G., Judith D. Tordoff and Mary Hilderman-Smith. *The Archaeology of the Royal Presidio of Santa Barbara: Phase VIII Archaeological Excavations of the Chapel Site*. Santa Barbara Trust for Historic Preservation, 1985.

Bolton, Herbert. *Anza's California Expeditions*. Vol. 5. University of California Press, 1930.

———. *Historical Memoirs of New California*. Vols. 1–4. Russell & Russell, 1926.

Brockington, Donald L. "The First Season's Work at the 'Silent City.'" *Journal of San Diego History* 17, no. 4 (1991).

Brockington, Donald L., and Raymond Brandes. "Mission San Diego de Alcalá: Archaeological and Historical Discoveries." *Some California Catholic Reminiscences for the United States Bicentennial*. California Catholic Conference, 1976.

Brown, Alan K. *A Description of Distant Roads*. San Diego State University Press, 2001.

Burrus, Ernest J., ed. *Diario del Capitan de Rivera y Moncada con un Apéndice Documental.* Colección Chimalistac Libros y Documento Acerca Nueva España, 24–25. Ediciones José Porras Turanzas, 1967.

Carrico, Richard L. "Castigating the Insolent Ones: Native Resistance and the Spanish Military, the Pa'mu Incident." *Journal of San Diego History* 64, no. 2 (2018).

———. "Death and Burial at the Royal Presidio de San Diego." *Pacific Coast Archaeological Society Quarterly* 55, no. 1 (2019).

———. "The Elephant and the Blind Men: Reflections on the Sestercentennial Commemoration." *Journal of San Diego History* 65, no. 2 (2019).

———. "Kumeyaay Crime and Punishment in Spanish San Diego 1769–1826." *Boletín: Journal of the California Mission Studies Association* 37, no. 1 (2021).

———. "Kumeyaay Inscriptive Art at Three Spanish Colonial Period Sites in San Diego: Cultural Continuity, Syncretic Behavior, or Resistive Art?" *Rock Art Papers* 19. San Diego Rock Art Association, 2018.

———. "Phantoms of the Past." *Boletín: Journal of the California Mission Studies Association* 39, no.1 (2023).

———. "Phoenix Buttons from the San Diego Presidio Chapel Complex Excavations." Manuscript on file at the San Diego History Center, San Diego, California, 1982.

———. "Phoenix Buttons from the Wrightington Adobe, Old Town San Diego." Manuscript on file with the Department of Parks and Recreation, 1990.

———. "The 1775 Sacking of Mission San Diego de Alcalá." *Journal of San Diego History* (Spring 1997).

———. "Spanish Crime and Punishment: The Native American Experience in Colonial San Diego, 1769–1830." *Western Legal History* 3, no. 1 (1990): 21–33.

———. "When Satan Stalked the Hills of Southern California: Diabolism in Colonial San Diego." Paper presented at the California Indian Conference, San Francisco, 1998.

Chace, Paul. "International Alliance—International Assault, Sovereign Kosaii Kumeyaay Perspectives on the Beginning of the Spanish Presidio-Mission at San Diego." Paper presented at the 2017 California Mission Foundation Conference, Mission Santa Inés, 2017.

Cheever, Dale. "An Historical Faunal Analysis: Large Mammal Utilization at the San Diego Presidio." Master's thesis, San Diego State University, 1983.

Cook, Sherburne F. "Smallpox in Spanish and Mexican California." *Bulletin of the History of Medicine* 7, no. 2 (1939): 153–91.

Costello, Julia. "Santa Ines Mission Excavations: 1986–1988." *Coyote Press Publications in California Historical Archaeology* no. 1 (1989).

Costello, Julia, and Davis Hornbeck. "Alta California: An Overview." In *Columbian Consequences*, vol. 1, edited by David H. Thomas. Smithsonian Institution Press, 1988.

Cuero, Delfina. *Autobiography of Delfina Cuero*. Translated by Rosalie Robertson and edited by Florence Shipek. Malki Museum Press, 1991.

Davis, James T. *Trade Routes of the Indians of California*. University of California Press, 1960.

Deagan, Kathleen. *Artifacts of the Spanish Colonies of Florida and the Caribbean 1500–1800*. Vol. 1: *Ceramics, Glassware, and Beads*. Smithsonian Institution Press, 1987.

Deetz, James. "Archaeological Excavations at La Purísima Mission." In *Historical Archaeology: A Guide to Substantive Theoretical Contributions*, edited by Robert Schuyler. Baywood Publishing Company, 1974, 160–90.

Dietler, John, Heather Gibson and James M. Potter. *Abundant Harvests: The Archaeology of Industry and Agriculture at San Gabriel Mission.* SWCA Anthropological Research Paper No. 11. SWCA Environmental Consultants, Pasadena, 2015.

Egenhoff, Elisabeth. *Fabricas*. Division of California Mines, 1952.

Englehardt, Zephyrin. *San Diego Mission.* James Barry Company, 1920.

Engstrand, Iris. "Letters of Pedro Fages." *Journal of San Diego History* 21, no. 2 (1975).

Ezell, Greta. "The Adobe Church of the Presidio of San Diego and Its Predecessor." *San Bernardino County Museum Association Quarterly* 54, no. 4 (2009): 17–43.

Ezell, Paul H. "The Excavation Program at the San Diego Presidio." *Journal of San Diego History* 22, no. 4 (1976): 1–20.

Ezell, Paul H., and Greta Ezell. "Bread and Barbeques at San Diego Presidio." In *Spanish Borderlands Research*, edited by Henry F. Dobyns. Center for Anthropological Studies, 1987.

Fitch, Henry Delano. "Documentos de Henry Fitch." Notes and manuscripts on file at the San Diego History Center. San Diego, California, 1848.

Godden, Geoffrey A. *Encyclopaedia of British Pottery and Porcelain Marks*. Schiffer Publishing, 1964.

———. *An Illustrated Encyclopedia of British Pottery and Porcelain*. Herbert Jenkins, 1966.

Graves, Clifford, et al., ed. "Cosoy, First Spanish Stop in Alta California." *Brand Book Number Eight*. Corral of the Westerners, 1980.

Griset, Suzanne. "Historic Transformations of Tizon Brown Ware in Southern California." In *Hunter-Gatherer Pottery from the Far West*. Edited by Joanne M. Mack. *Nevada State Museum Anthropological Papers* no. 23. 1990.

Guest, Francis. "Mission Colonization and Political Control in Spanish California." *Journal of San Diego History* 24, no. 1 (1978): 97–116.

Hackel, Steven. *Children of Coyote, Missionaries of Saint Francis: Indian Spanish Relations in Colonial California*. University of North Carolina Press, 2005.

———. "Glass Beads and the Village of Guaspet." In *People in a Changing Land: The Archaeology and History of the Ballona in Los Angeles, California 5. Gabrielino/Tongva origins and Development. A View from Guaspet*, edited by John G. Douglass, Seetha N. Reedy, Richard Ciolet-Torell and Donn Grenda. Scientific Research, 2016.

Hedges, Kenneth. "Kumeyaay: A Problem of Identification." *Journal of California Anthropology* 5, no. 2 (1978).

Heizer, Robert F. "Impact of Colonization on the Native California Societies." *Journal of San Diego History* 24, no. 1 (1978): 121–40.

Hoover, Robert L., and Julia Costello, eds. "Excavations at Mission San Antonio, 1976–1978." *Institute of Archaeology, Monograph* 26. University of California–Los Angeles, 1985.

Howard, Don M. *The Royal Presidio of Monterey: Architectural Documentation and Archaeology.* Monterey County Archaeological Society, 1978.

Howard, Jeffrey. "Description of the Human Remains from the Presidio, San Diego." Master's thesis, San Diego State University, 1975.

Inventario Mision San Diego. "Inventory of the Goods, Livestock and Buildings at Mission San Diego for the Years Beginning in 1777–1783." Untranslated manuscript, Archivos de Californias, Bancroft Library, Berkeley, 1777.

Jackson, Robert F., and Edward Castillo. *Indians, Franciscans, and Spanish Colonization*. University of New Mexico Press, 1995.

Jackson, Robert H. *Indian Population Decline: The Missions of Northwestern New Spain, 1687–1840*. University of New Mexico Press, 1994.

Jayme, Luis. *Letters of Luis Jayme, O.F.M., San Diego, October 17, 1772*. Maynard Geiger, trans. and ed. Dawson's Book Shop, 1970.

Kenneally, Finabar. *Writings of Fermín Francisco de Lasuen*. Vol. 1. Academy of American Franciscan History, 1965.

Kirk, Myrle A. "Buttons from the San Buenaventura Mission Site." In *3500 Years on One City Block, San Buenaventura Mission Plaza Project Archaeological Report*, edited by Roberta S. Greenwood. Redevelopment Agency, City of San Buenaventura, 1975.

———. "Buttons from the San Buenaventura Mission Site, 1975." In *The Changing Faces of Main Street*, edited by Roberta S. Greenwood. Redevelopment Agency, City of San Buenaventura, 1976.

Krase, Jean. "The Old World Ceramic Sherds from San Diego's Presidio: A Qualitative, Quantitative and Historical Analysis." Thesis, San Diego State University, 1979.

———. "Ships and Sherds: Ceramics at the San Diego Presidio." *Journal of San Diego History* 27, no. 2 (1981): 129–41.

Lee, Georgia, and Norman Neuerburg. "The Alta California Indians as Artists." In *Columbian Consequences*, vol. 1, edited by David H. Thomas. Smithsonian Institution Press, 1989.

Lennert, Ellen Gooley. "X-Rays and Artifacts at the San Diego Presidio Excavations." *Journal of San Diego History* 18, no. 5 (1973): 22–24.

Lister, Florence C., and Robert H. Lister. "Maiolica in Colonial Spanish America." *Historical Archaeology* 8 (1974): 17–52.

Livingston, Milla. "The Only Phoenix I Have Ever Had/The Story of the Phoenix Button/The Phoenix." *Michigan Button Bulletin* 18, no. 2 (1960): 2–4.

Luomala, Katherine. "Tipai and Ipai." *Handbook of North American Indians*. Vol. 8. Smithsonian Institution Press, 1978.

Mason, William M. "The Garrisons of San Diego Presidio 1770–1794." *Journal of San Diego History* 24, no. 4 (1978).

May, Ronald V. "Mexican Majolica at the Presidio of Monterey." *Monterey County Archaeological Society Quarterly* 3, no. 4 (1974): 1–6.

———. "A Southern California Indigenous Ceramic Typology: A Contribution to Malcolm J. Rogers Research." *Journal of the Archaeological Survey Association of Southern California* 2, no. 2 (1978): 1–54.

Miskwish, Michael Connolly. *Maay Uuyow: Kumeyaay Cosmology*. Shuluk, 2016.

Moriarty, James R. "Excavations at Mission San Diego." *Masterkey* 45, no. 4 (1971): 124–37.

———. "Historic Site Archaeology at Mission San Diego." *Masterkey* 43, no. 3 (1969): 99–108.

———. "With His Boots On." *Masterkey* 47, no. 2 (1973): 54–61.

Moriarty, James R., and Brian Smith. "Discovery and Interpretation of Intaglio Impressions: Mission San Diego de Alcalá." *Pacific Coast Archaeological Society Quarterly* 13, no. 4 (1977): 67–72.

Moriarty, James R., and William R. Weyland. "Excavations at San Diego Mission." *Masterkey* 45, no. 4 (1971): 124–37.

Neuerburg, Norman. "The Changing Face of Mission San Diego." *Journal of San Diego History* 32, no. 1 (1986): 1–26.

Ortega, José Francisco. "Insurrección de Indios, Resultado Castigo de Cabecillas." April 6, 1778. *Provincial State Papers, Benicia Military* vol. 1, 1778.

———. "Revolt of the Indians, Burning of the Mission, Death of the Missionary, November 30, 1775." In the Provincial State Papers, Benicia, Military, Vol. 1, 1775.

Palou, Francisco. *Historical Memoirs of New California.* Vol. 4. Edited by Herbert E. Bolton. Russell & Russell, 1966.

Panich, Lee M. "Archaeologies of Persistence: Reconsidering the Legacies of Colonialism in Native North America." *American Antiquity* 78, no. 1 (2013): 105–22.

———. "Beyond the Colonial Curtain: Investigating Indigenous Use of Obsidian in Spanish California Through the XRF Analysis of Artifacts from Mission Santa Clara." *Journal of Archaeological Science* 5 (2016): 521–30.

———. "Missionization and the Persistence of Native Identity on the Colonial Frontier of Baja California." *Ethnohistory* 57 (2010): 225–62.

———. "Native American Consumption of Shell and Glass Beads at Mission Santa Clara de Assi." *American Antiquity* 79, no. 4 (2014): 730–48.

———. "'Sometimes They Bury the Deceased's Clothes and Trinkets': Indigenous Mortuary Practices at Mission Santa Clara de Assi." *Historical Archaeology* 49, no. 4 (2015): 110–29.

Panich, Lee, and T.D. Schneider. "Expanding Mission Archaeology: A Landscape Approach to Indigenous Autonomy in Colonial California." *Journal of Anthropological Archaeology* 40 (2015): 48–58.

Pattie, James Ohio. *The Personal Narrative of James O. Pattie.* Reprinted Arno Press, 1973; Arcadia Press, 2007.

Pechell, G.R. *A Visit to the Capital and Chief Ports of the Isle of St. Domingo.* Mottley & Harrison, 1824.

Porcayo, Antonio Michelini. "The Immaculate Conception, Father Junípero Serra, and the Bifacial Crucifixes of San Fernando Velicatá, Baja California." *Boletín: Journal of the California Mission Studies Association* 31, no. 1 (2015): 145–58.

Preston, J.C. "Serpent in Eden: Dispersal of Foreign Diseases into Pre-Mission California." *Journal of San Diego History* 18, no. 1 (1996): 2–37.

Ross, Lester. "Analysis of Glass Beads from Santa Ines Mission. Santa Ines Mission Excavations: 1986–1988." In *Publications in California Historical Archaeology*, edited by Julia Costello. Coyote Press, 1989.

Rudolph, Cathy. Listing of Phoenix Buttons Found at the Santa Barbara Presidio Excavation. E-mail to Richard Carrico, February 24, 1996.

San Diego Presidio Chapel Excavation Catalog. Collections Management Department, San Diego State University Department of Anthropology, 2005.

Sasson, Aharon, and Susan Arter. "Earliest Utilization of Chicken in Upper California: The Zooarchaeology of Avian Remains from the San Diego Royal Presidio." *American Antiquity* 85, no. 3 (2020): 516–34.

Shipek, Florence. "Saints or Oppressors: The Franciscan Missionaries of California." *The Missions of California: A Legacy of Genocide.* Indian Historian Press, 1987.

Sorensen, Cloyd, Jr., and C. Richard Le Roy. "Trade Beads: The Powerful Companion of the Explorer." *Brand Book Number One*. San Diego Corral of the Westerners, 1968.

Sprague, Roderick. "Glass Trade Beads: A Progress Report." *Historical Archaeology* 19, no. 2 (1985): 87–105.

———. "The Literature of the Phoenix Button." Unpublished manuscript in the possession of the author. University of Idaho–Moscow, 1991.

Strong, Emory. "Enigma of the Phoenix Button." *Historical Archaeology* 9 (1975): 74–80.

———. "Phoenix Buttons." *American Antiquity* 25, no. 3 (1960): 418–19.

Temple, Tomas W. "Two Letters from Sergeant Jose Francisco Ortega to Governor Felipe de Neve, September 4 and 5, 1781." *Historical Society of Southern California Quarterly* 22, no. 4 (1940): 121–30.

Tibesar, Antonine. *Writings of Junipero Serra*. Vols. 1–3. Edited by Antonine Tibesar. Academy of American Franciscan History, 1925.

Torrent, Hilario. Letter from Hilario Torrent to Francisco Palou, November 27, 1788. Folio 44–47, *Fondo Franciscano.* Vol. 67. Instituto Nacional de Antropolgia y Historia (INAH), México City, 1788.

Trafzer, Clifford. "Serra's Legacy: The Desecration of American Indian Burials at Mission San Diego." *American Indian Culture and Research Journal* 16, no. 2 (1992): 57–75.

Van Wormer, Stephen. "An Analysis of Glass Artifacts from the Chapel Complex Excavation at the Presidio of San Diego." *Pacific Coast Archaeological Society Quarterly* 50, nos. 1–2 (2014).

Van Wormer, Stephen, Sue Wade and Susan Walter. *Shadows of the Things That Have Been: An Analysis of and Identification Guide to Ceramics from the Chapel Complex Excavation of the San Diego Presidio.* 2024. Available through Academia online.

Wilken-Robertson, Michael. *Kumeyaay Ethnobotany: Shared Heritage of the Californias*. Sunbelt Publications, n.d.

Williams, Jack. "San Diego Presidio: A Vanished Military Community of Upper California." *Presidios of the North American Spanish Borderlands*, Society for Historical Archaeology 38, no. 3 (2004).

ABOUT THE AUTHOR

Richard Carrico is an award-winning author of nonfiction and historical fiction with a focus on Spanish borderlands archaeology, Indigenous people and true crime. Richard grew up in San Diego and attended elementary, middle school (called junior high at the time) and San Diego High School before serving in the U.S. Army in the late 1960s. From a young age, he has been fascinated by the San Diego Presidio and its history.

Richard holds a BA in history from San Diego State College and a BA in anthropology from San Diego State University. As a postgraduate, he earned an MA in history from the University of San Diego. Richard taught history, anthropology and Native American studies at San Diego State University for thirty years before retiring in 2024.

For more than forty years, Richard participated in archaeological studies in California, Baja California, Arizona and Hawaii. He directed the San Diego Presidio excavations for two seasons and conducted research on the site for more than forty-five years. That research took Richard to major archival institutions in California, Mexico City and Washington, D.C. For his research and contributions to California history, Richard was awarded the prestigious California Missions Foundation Norman Neuerburg Award for outstanding contributions to the study of California missions and presidios.

Richard has authored more than twenty academic articles that appeared in professional journals and at least twenty articles in popular magazines, including *SkyWest Spirit*, *San Diego Home & Garden*, *San Diego Reader* and *Ranch & Coast Magazine*. He has published five books on a variety of topics.

This book is his second publication with Arcadia Publishing/The History Press. His book *Ramona*, in the Images of America series, was a well-received portrayal of a rural community. His *Strangers in a Stolen Land*, the story of San Diego County's Native Americans, is used as a textbook at several universities. Richard's most recent book, *Monsters on the Loose*, won second place at the 2024 Book Fest and was a Silver Falchion Award Finalist at the 2024 Killer Nashville event. His short story "Animals Who Talk, Sing, and Dance" received an Honorable Mention Award from *Writer's Digest Magazine*. His most recent piece, "Habla Espanol? If You Rodeo You Do" was published in *Cowboy Up* rodeo magazine.